The Hali'imaile General Store Cookbook

THE HALI'IMAILE GENERAL STORE COOKBOOK

Home Cooking from Maui

Beverly Gannon

with Bonnie Friedman

Dessert Recipes by Teresa Gannon

Photography by Laurie Smith

TEN SPEED PRESS
Berkeley / Toronto

🔟

Ten Speed Press
PO Box 7123
Berkeley, California 94707
www.tenspeed.com

Distributed in Australia by Simon and Schuster Australia, in Canada by Ten Speed Press Canada, in New Zealand by Southern Publishers Group, in South Africa by Real Books, and in the United Kingdom and Europe by Publishers Group UK.

Cover and Text Design by Nancy Austin
Food and Prop Styling by Wesley Martin, San Francisco
Paintings pages i and 196 by Pam Hayes (photo by Rob Ratkowski)
Photograph page 195 © 1999 by Steve Brinkman
Prop Styling page 195 by Gail Simmons

Library of Congress Cataloging-in-Publication Data
Gannon, Beverly, 1949–
The Hali'imaile General Store cookbook : home cooking from Maui / Beverly Gannon with Bonnie Friedman ; dessert recipes by Teresa Gannon.
p. cm.
ISBN-10: 1-58008-170-3 (cloth)
ISBN-13: 978-1-58008-170-2 (cloth)
1. Cookery, Hawaiian.   2. Cookery—Hawaii—Maui.   3. Hali'imaile General Store (Restaurant).
I. Friedman, Bonnie, 1951–   II. Hali'imaile General Store (Restaurant).   III. Title.
TX724.5.H3 G36   2000
641.59969—dc21   00-032572

Printed in China

7 8 9 10 11 — 11 10 09 08 07

For all those people who've eaten at the restaurant and begged and pleaded for recipes so that they can go home to Wisconsin, Florida, or Louisiana, and easily re-create the dishes they loved at Hali'imaile. I've always told those patrons, "One of these days, I'll do a book." Well, folks, here it is! And I hope every single copy gets food-stained, dog-eared, used over and over again, and most of all, enjoyed.

CONTENTS

ACKNOWLEDGMENTS

Where do I begin? There are so many people who have contributed to the success of Hali'imaile General Store. First, there would be no Hali'imaile General Store without the hundreds of employees that have come and gone over the past twelve years. Each individual left his or her imprint, making up the complex and ever-changing character of the store.

A multitude of *mahalo:*

To my investors, Shep Gordon, Richard and Lauren Shuler Donner, Steve and Rose North, Tom Collins, and the Joseph sisters, for helping to finance my dream. You made me richer with your trust. I only wish I could have made you richer with your investment. Maybe next time.

To Colin Cameron, who believed in me before I believed in myself. I miss you.

To Doug MacCluer for tolerating my need to always get my way. You're the best landlord one could have.

To Paul Meyer for all your support. You were a believer even through your doubts.

To Eunice Garcia and Sylvia Hunt for all your help with historical information and photos from the archives.

To Richard Roderick and David Perlini, who came to work for me in the "converted garage" kitchen. Little did you suspect you would be involved in the birth of a catering business turned take-out food shop turned restaurant. Thank you for the crash, hands-on course in Restaurant Business 101.

In the restaurant business, you need someone you can trust completely to make sure that a piece of fish or a handful of bananas does not "walk out" the back door. Big Larry, you have been watching my back for almost twelve years. You call me "Ma." I call you "Son." I took you by the hand to a rehab center ten years ago and saved your life. You now save mine every day.

What would I do without Tom Lelli? You are the cornerstone of the kitchen. You understand the level of taste I demand in my food. You know how to translate my ideas into the menu, and your creativity is evident in every menu change. Your passion for what you do extends to each dish that is placed on a table. You make me very proud of every morsel of food that comes out of the kitchen.

To Shaun Waite, Scott Idemoto, Edwin Santos, Kris Sugihara, Brandon Shim, Dominic Paonas, and Paul Lamparelli. You are an awesome support team. Each of you brings your own style and creativity to the kitchen. To Joe Plansei, Sharleen Passkiewicz, and Dave Ferreira. The kitchen would be a mess without you.

To my old, dear friend Rebecca Schillaci. You instinctively know me so well, that you run Hali'imaile General Store exactly the way I want it run. I have entrusted you with my "first-born," and I have never regretted it for a moment. I hope you are well planted in Olinda, for "you can check out any time you like but you can never leave."

Twelve years later, Joanie Jolley is still talking about retiring. We will not let her. You were the first "floor" staff we hired, for part-time work. You helped clean the store before we opened. Then came Debbie Mercado, Lorie Bolte, Julie McDermott, Carol Schramm, Tim Jones, Stacy Wood, and Tina Russell. You have all been around longer than we care to remember.

To Patrice, Julie, Miya, Annie, and Shye for making sure over the years everyone gets paid!

To the "great" Henry Blenner. If you ever quit, I shall quit, too. You have become an indispensable part of my business and my life. Move over, Joe.

To my assistant, Jayanne Jefferys, for wanting to learn how to be "me" so that I do not have to work so hard. That is the greatest compliment I have ever had. Now if you could just learn how to cook!

To my daughters, Cheech, Cathy, and Jana, for making Hali'imaile a "family affair." You all make me so proud. I love you more than you can imagine. You are my treasures.

To my co-author, Bonnie Friedman. Let's face it. The book is here because of you. For me, the most wonderful part about the whole process was watching our friendship flourish. I plan on continuing "Sundays with Bonnie" and having Joe pamper us with lox, eggs, and onions. *Mahalo mai ku'u pu'uwai.* It was a great experience.

To Phil Wood, Jo Ann Deck, Lorena Jones, and Holly Taines White at Ten Speed Press. Thank you all for giving me the opportunity to fulfill one of my life's goals. You made something I thought would be difficult, easier.

To Laurie Smith, Wes Martin, and Nancy Austin for making my food look so appetizing, and for caring enough to make the finished product so perfect. You are an awesome team.

To Barbara Fitzpatrick for even giving up your birthday to finish typing the recipes. We shall drink that bottle of Dom Perignon soon!

Countless artist friends, neighbors, and even one of our former cooks have displayed their art in the restaurant over the years. Everyone is an upcountry neighbor. We consider each one a Calabash Cousin, a local term of endearment for friends who are more like family. We are grateful to them all. Four have been central to Hali'imaile General Store since the beginning—floral designer Masako Westcott, ceramist Karen Jennings, sculptor Tom Faught, and painter Jan Kasprzycki. You'll see samples of their work in each section of the book.

I have left the most important thank you for last. To the love of my life, my husband, Joe Gannon. You were unaware when you married me twenty years ago that you would have to share me with my secret passion. And you have braved the years with undaunting support. You are my biggest fan and my greatest support. You allow me to be my intense, crazy self, and have learned to just "go with my flow." You bring me coffee in bed, rub my tired feet, lend me your shoulder to cry on, and wipe away my tears. You are truly the "perfect mate." Thank you for putting up with me all these years. I love you more every day.

I now know how it would feel to make one of those acceptance speeches at an awards show. There is not enough time or space to thank everyone, but as they say, you all know who you are and I thank you all from the bottom of my heart.

INTRODUCTION

THE GANNON FAMILY

Looking back at my family life—both my growing up in Dallas and the twenty-plus years since Joe and I were married—I probably shouldn't be surprised that I ended up in this business. I was raised in the Jewish tradition of "eat, eat, eat." It's what got me interested in food and its preparation. I think it's still what people want: the kind of warm, comforting food that came out of "Mom's kitchen," provided, of course, that Mom was a good cook!

Before embarking on a culinary career, I was road manager for Liza Minelli, Joey Heatherton, and Ben Vereen. After five years, I realized it was time to get serious about my life, and I went off to Le Cordon Bleu in London and then took classes with Marcella Hazan and Jacques Pépin.

When I returned to Dallas, I worked for a caterer for a short time before starting my own catering company. In 1980, I bumped into a man I'd met briefly seven years earlier. But this time it was love at first sight. We moved to Maui several months later, then shortly after that, we married.

Joe Gannon is a lighting designer by trade and a producer—by necessity—of mega-rock 'n' roll shows. His show business friends and clients were my first "customers." Whenever any of them planned a trip to Maui, someone back in Los Angeles or New York would tell them, "Call Beverly. She'll cook for you." Just about every one of them did! After five years, I thought, "Maybe I can make a living at this." I started catering "officially" in May 1985 under the company name Fresh Approach. Today, we call the catering division Celebrations, because that's really what we do: plan and execute celebrations of every size and description.

Our three daughters, at one time or another, have all been involved in our business. Two are very much a part of it today, as is Joe, who handles the financial end of the business, keeps the wine list in shape, and often "works the room" during service.

Our oldest daughter, Cathy, came to Maui in 1984, to get married and moved here with her husband two years later. Cathy had worked as a server and bartender for years in California so she knew much more about the restaurant business than I did. It was great that she was here when we opened Hali'imaile. Her husband worked on the construction of the store and she became our bar manager. She stopped working when she became pregnant with our first grandson, Tyler, in 1990, and then came back to work at the restaurant in 1998 as a bar and day manager. It's nice to know that a family member is keeping their eye on the business.

Jana, the youngest, moved to Maui with us in 1980. After she graduated from high school in 1984, she'd often help with catering, usually doing prep work. Jana was in a serious car accident right around Thanksgiving 1986. She broke both her wrists and was in casts above her elbows. New Year's Eve that year I had both a small party and a big party to cater. The big party needed all the staff I knew of on the island at that

time. So I sent Jana and a friend's daughter to do the small party. Imagine her carrying trays of food *on* her casts! Only a family member would be that devoted. Jana is now married with two children and lives in Los Angeles, where her husband, Greg, is a screenwriter/director.

Middle daughter Teresa, affectionately known as Cheech to family and friends, is our pastry chef. She began baking as a little girl with her grandmother and was soon making cookies and pies for Joe's rock 'n' roll soirées. She turned "pro" in the early 1980s at Charmer's Market in Los Angeles and also worked with pastry chefs from Michael's Restaurant and L'Orangerie, both in Los Angeles.

Then Teresa packed up her pastry bags and headed to Europe for a couple of years. She worked for the famed Roux brothers at their three-star Michelin restaurant Le Gavroche in London, and after a short course at the highly acclaimed French pastry school, École Le Nôtre, she decided to stay in France to work and study.

Eventually, she brought her new and improved skills back to Los Angeles, where was the pastry chef at Le Chardonnay and Champagne. When we opened the store, she worked with us for the first three years and then went to New York and San Francisco to broaden her experience still further. But I guess there's no place like home. She came back to Hali'imaile in 1998, and I'm not sure who's happier, her parents or our customers.

Teresa has come into her own these last few years, and we're very proud that she's generally acknowledged to be one of Hawai'i's best pastry chefs. I think you'll enjoy getting to know Cheech through her wonderful desserts and the notes that introduce them.

I would be remiss if I didn't include in this introduction a bit about the family home. It's been a gathering place for the Gannon family and friends since we moved into it in 1982. Cathy's wedding was here, Jana's wedding was here, and Cheech's wedding was here, and it was also an integral part of the Hali'imaile pineapple plantation.

The house was built by C.W. Dickey, arguably Hawai'i's finest architect, in 1936 for the plantation's field superintendent, William Tuttle. Mr. Tuttle was an innovator who changed the pineapple industry in Hawai'i by, literally, changing the shape of the pineapple. Pineapples used to be round, and a lot of the fruit was lost in the canning process because the shape was not compatible with the equipment. Mr. Tuttle found a way to create the "square-shoulder" pineapple we know today through changing the DNA of the fruit.

Mr. Tuttle died in 1981, but he continued to live in our home until his wife died in 1997, at the age of ninety-nine. It's obvious to us, and to anyone familiar with this house, that he was waiting here for his wife to join him. Until the time of Mrs. Tuttle's death, every single person who ever stayed in this house asked if it had a spirit in it. Lest you think I'm crazy, let me assure you this is a very common thing in Hawai'i. As a matter of fact, by law you must disclose any spiritual activity on your property if you put it on the market for sale. Once you've lived with a spirit in your house, there is no question that the feeling of a presence of some kind is real. We would always walk in the house and say, "Hi, Mr. Tuttle, we're back." (We still say it, but now it refers to our cat named Mr. Tuttle, in tribute to our home's previous owner.)

I remember the very first "spiritual" thing that ever happened to me here. I was alone. We rarely close bedroom doors in this house. I went upstairs and our bedroom door was closed, the bedroom windows were totally steamed up, the bathroom windows were totally steamed up, and the hot water was on full blast. Hello, Mr. Tuttle!

Mr. Tuttle's presence was felt most fully in the middle bedroom. His grandson came into the store one day and, in the course of conversation, told me something I hadn't known before: the middle bedroom had been his grandfather's. I think his presence was one of the reasons I never felt afraid here, even when alone. There was always someone else here with me.

Anyway, I wanted this house from the first time I saw it because of its big, old plantation-style kitchen. I didn't care what the rest of the house looked like. I wanted a place to cook. Well, not a whole lot of cooking goes on here anymore, but the house is less than five minutes away from the store. There are days when I go back and forth six and eight times. Believe me, we would never have opened the store if we didn't live in this house.

The Place, the Plantation, the Store

Names are very important in Hawaiian culture, and place names usually provide at least some information about the locale itself. Hali'imaile is a good example. The Hawaiian word *hali'i* means "a covering" or "blanket." *Maile* is a native twining shrub with wonderfully fragrant, shiny leaves. They are used to make prized lei for special

occasions, like weddings, and for special people, like an esteemed elder, teacher, or a clergyman performing a blessing for a new home or business. We can assume—and we can only assume since Hawaiian was a strictly oral tradition until the 1820s—that in ancient times Hali'imaile was an area strewn with *maile*.

We may also assume that the ancients grew one of their most important dietary staples, sweet potatoes, or *'uala* as they are called in Hawaiian, in the area. There is a story about Chief Kiha'api'ilani, who, during a famine in Kula and Makawao, gathered potato slips from Hali'imaile and Hamakuapoko, took them up the mountain, and planted them. As soon as the slips were in the ground, it began to rain, providing all the water necessary for the new shoots to grow.

Located about twelve hundred feet up the slopes of Mount Haleakalā, Hali'imaile is, however, best known for its pineapple plantation and its plantation "village." According to a building account prepared for Maui Agricultural Company's Pineapple Department in 1931, the camp houses, as the workers' residences were called, were built in 1923 and 1924. The Hali'imaile Plantation Store, at the time a branch of Maui Ag's Pā'ia Store and run by the company, was built in 1925, with an extension added in 1927. Total cost of the building and the extension, including all the fixtures, was less than seventy-five hundred dollars!

Typical plantation communities were self-contained, and Hali'imaile was no exception. In addition to the store and the houses, the company built and operated a gymnasium, dispensary, theater, scout hall, garage, and office.

Plantation stores were not just grocery stores, of course. The Hali'imaile Store, or Superette, as it was commonly called by camp residents, had a butcher shop, a fish market, and a post office inside and sold clothing and household appliances in addition to groceries. In the early days, residents could buy any cut of meat, including T-bone steaks, for twenty-five cents a pound. According to oral histories taken in the 1980s by Maui Land & Pineapple Company, "for $20 you could fill the bed of your pick-up" with groceries.

Eventually Maui Ag evolved into Maui Pineapple Company, which took over operation of the Hali'imaile Store on January 1, 1947. Nine years later, according to company records, Maui Pineapple Company, Limited, entered into a ten-year lease agreement with the Shimoda brothers. Rent for the first year for the store, the store

porch, two warehouses—one a quonset type—a shed, and the garage was three hundred dollars. The price increased for the last nine years of the lease to six hundred dollars a year, payable in "equal monthly installments of $50." It was at that time that the store became known as the Hali'imaile Super Market and the equipment list that accompanied the lease included such items as a meat scale, meat band saw, meat slicer, meat grinder, meat chopping block, two meat tables, a fish sink, and a potato bin.

After the term of the Shimoda brothers' lease, several people tried to make a go of the store, according to a number of oral histories. At some point during those intervening years, one leaseholder or another changed the name to the Hali'imaile General Store. Upcountry residents in the 1970s and '80s remember it as a not-very-well-stocked place to stop for a six-pack of soda, a roll of paper towels, or a pack of cigarettes and not much more. But that would all change in 1988.

To this day, I call Hali'imaile General Store, "the store." Rarely, if ever, do I refer to it as "the restaurant." I'll tell anyone who'll listen to me that I never, ever intended to be in the restaurant business. But sometimes you just don't have a choice.

It was Christmastime 1987 when we heard that the Hali'imaile General Store was going to be available for rent. We thought it would work perfectly as a combination gourmet take-out deli, catering headquarters, and general store, with a few tables where people could snack while they were waiting for their take-out order. After almost six months of negotiations, we finally signed the lease. Everyone thought we were crazy, opening a place, literally, in the middle of a thousand-acre pineapple plantation. But remember, we weren't opening a restaurant. We just needed a great space from which to run our catering operation.

We had lots of excellent help as we set out refurbishing the building. With drawings by Joe's good friend, Hollywood set and production designer Jerimy Railton, the renovation team preserved much of the old charm. That included 70 percent of the original Philippine mahogany floor, which remains today. Joe, of course, took care of all the lighting.

The day we opened, October 14, 1988, there were a hundred people waiting to get in. We had five or six tables, maybe thirty chairs, no wait staff, and everyone who came in the door asked, "Where do we sit?" Hali'imaile General Store is a restaurant, in large part, because that's what our customers wanted it to be.

We have two dining rooms, and, yes, there are plenty of tables and chairs for everyone. The front dining room, with its high ceilings, exhibition kitchen, and towering pine shelves stocked full of giftware and

gourmet foods, is the place to see and be seen. You never know when you'll spot Alice Cooper, Arnold Schwarzenegger, or Sharon Stone. Our back dining room is quieter, more softly lit, more intimate. Over the years that back room has been the site of more birthday parties, retirement parties, bon voyage parties, and wedding rehearsal dinners than I care to count. When I think back to the very beginning, I still laugh . . . and cry.

We'd been open less than one week. A waiter was bringing a piece of chocolate macadamia nut pie with whipped cream to a table. Somewhere between the pantry and the table, a fly landed in the whipped cream, unbeknownst to the waiter. I was mortified. I asked the customer what I could do to make him happy, "Can I buy you dinner? Can I put your kids through college?" My stomach was in knots, tears welled up in my eyes, I was embarrassed, and I was heartbroken, and I vowed never, ever, ever to serve another piece of chocolate macadamia nut pie again.

Well, thousands and thousands and thousands of pieces of pie later, my stomach doesn't knot up, I don't cry, and I don't break out in hives when we make a mistake. But I still do take it personally because I want my guests to be completely satisfied at all costs. I think it's a primal thing—a woman thing. On one side of the coin, I believe that's why I may not be the greatest

businessperson in the world. On the other side of the coin, I still care enough about each customer to do everything in my power to ensure a great experience at Hali'imaile.

We've been fortunate over the years to receive some wonderful recognition locally, nationally, and internationally, in newspapers, magazines, and books. Such recognition is very nice, but my focus remains our food. We've been serving good food for more than a decade, and we plan to do that very thing for a long, long time to come. Some of our dishes have truly become classics here at Hali'imaile, so we've marked those recipes throughout the book, so that you can enjoy these quintessential preparations.

I believe in feeding people great food and lots of it. You have to make customers smile. You have to make them go "Mmmmm." You have to make sure they leave the table satisfied. I believe that's what we've done over the years, and I think it is the main reason for our success. In spite of the long hours, and the fact that I continue to deny that I'm in the restaurant business, I'm very proud of how far we—and I personally—have come.

HAWAI'I THROUGH THE SEASONS

The vast majority of our visitors—even in this sophisticated age—believe we have one season in Hawai'i, the proverbial Endless Summer. It is surely part of the paradise fantasy that lives in the imaginations of those who dream of coming here. Every upcountry resident on any of our islands will tell you, it's just not so, and the longer you live here, the more distinct the seasons become. Especially obvious are the vast differences between winter and summer.

The air warms and the entire midsection of Haleakalā is engulfed in an extraordinary purple haze. It's spring and the jacaranda trees are in full bloom. Grown-ups shed their sweaters and jackets. Children say bye-bye to their closed shoes and begin living in their rubber slippers. Yards and gardens are tended in earnest.

Ah, summer! Mango and lychee trees are so heavily laden with fruits that their branches are in peril of snapping. Neighbors exchange brown-paper grocery sacks full of fruit, and in particularly good years, card-board boxes marked "Free Mangos" and "Free Lychees" are left on sidewalks and roadsides so anyone without a tree can enjoy the wealth.

The heady aromas of guava and white ginger mingle to fill the air on a Sunday drive to the town of Hāna on Maui's windward coast. You bring a few stalks of torch ginger to a friend's home. But you'll never reveal your secret place for collecting these amazing blooms. It is unmistakably fall and time to buy new school supplies and maybe even a new sweater.

One winter in the early 1990s, the snow (yes, the *snow!*) on top of ten-thousand-foot Mount Haleakalā reached all the way down to the seven-thousand-foot level, something no one here could remember ever having seen before. Local families dug out whatever warm clothing they had kept on hand (usually in a box in the carport, for the occasional mainland trip), bundled up the kids, got in the family truck or van, and took the long drive up to Haleakalā National Park for what may have been a once-in-a-lifetime snowball fight. Granted, we don't outfit our cars with snow tires and the temperature rarely dips below 55 degrees or so down at sea level. But believe me, even downcountry residents pull out their extra blankets at 55 or 60 degrees. We mountain dwellers enjoy gathering around a roaring fire at Christmastime as much as the mainlanders do. And most of us wouldn't dream of getting into the ocean during the winter months. The exceptions, of course, are the surfers who live for the big waves on the north shores and the humpback whales who winter here. The water is certainly warmer than in their native Alaska!

We are fortunate here to have a bounty of fine food products with which to work all year long. But having an upcountry restaurant affords us the opportunity to make the most on our menu of the seasonal differences, subtle though they may sometimes appear.

In spring and summer, our guests enjoy lighter fare. More salads, light pasta and fish preparations, lots of tropical fruits, and fresh-from-the-field vegetables make up most of our menu from March to September.

With the first hint of a chill in the mountain air come the flavors of fall. We feature pumpkin, corn, duck, nuts, and berries on every section of our menu.

On our winter menu, we offer hearty, stick-to-your-ribs dishes like thick soups, stews, and red meats. It's also the best season to enjoy some of our local fishes, such as monchong, onaga, and ahi. Gingerbread, bread pudding, layer cakes, and cream pies fill our dessert tray. We have arranged our recipes by season so that you can experience, albeit vicariously, the wonderful annual subtleties enjoyed by those of us lucky enough to live here.

Before we get to the recipes, a word about one of them. I think I've had more requests for my crab dip recipe than all other recipes combined. It's also one of very few recipes I've never shared. I suspect everyone who knows me—and who loves me for my crab dip—will expect to find it in this book. I guess you'll all just have to read on and see.

Spring Recipes to Awaken
the Imagination

APPETIZERS

Smoked Salmon Bundles with Spicy Shrimp and Lomilomi Tomato Salsa, 5

Hamachi with Sizzling Oil, Seaweed Salad, and Ponzu Sauce, 6

Seafood Martini with Wasabi-Ginger Cocktail Sauce, 7

Terrine of Kula Vegetables with Roasted Tomato Vinaigrette, 8

SOUPS

Curried Squash Soup, 10

Maui Onion and Ginger Soup, 11

Carrot-Ginger Soup, 12

SALADS

Asian Pear and Duck Tostada, 13

Soba Noodle Salad with Passion Fruit Vinaigrette, 15

Niçoise Salad with a Toss, 16

Rock Shrimp and Crab Cakes with Baby Spinach and Mango Mayonnaise, 17

ENTRÉES

Coulibiac of Opakapaka with Passion Fruit Hollandaise, 18

Salmon Strudel, 21

Mixed Grill of Hawaiian Snapper with Chardonnay Sauce, 22

Crab Cannelloni with Lemongrass-Ginger Sauce, 23

Sesame-Crusted Mahimahi with Coconut-Curry Cabbage and Rum-Baked Bananas, 24

Shrimp and Scallop Stir-Fry with Pineapple Fried Rice, 27

Ancho Chile–Marinated Uku with Corn Salsa and Ginger Cream, 29

Angel Hair Pasta with Tomatoes, Basil, and Pine Nuts, 30

Smoked Chicken Tortelloni with a Trio of Mustard Cream Sauce, 31

Crunchy Macadamia Nut Chicken over Tropical Fruit Paella, 32

Spicy Coconut Lobster and Shrimp over Soba Noodles, 34

Shrimp, Duck Sausage, and Goat Cheese Pasta, 35

Desserts

Piña Colada Cheesecake, 37

Liliko'i, Guava, and White Chocolate Cheesecake, 38

Guava-Raspberry Crème Brûlée, 39

Double Coconut Cream Cake, 40

Kula Strawberry Shortcake, 43

Lemon Crepes with Raspberry Compote, 44

Soon after I moved to Maui, I started to shop at Ooka's, a small, local-style supermarket. Five-gallon buckets filled with anthuriums and obaki and all kinds of exotic flowers were always offered for sale. The bunches were tied together in incredible ways, so that when you got home you could just untie them, put the flowers in a vase, and they would look fabulous. I'm not good at arranging flowers, so these bouquets were the solution for me. I asked the checkers where they came from and was told about Masako.

One day Masako and I happened to be shopping at the same time. I asked her if she did arrangements for parties, which she did.

We soon found we enjoyed working together, and from the day I opened, I've had Masako's extraordinary arrangements in the restaurant. I look at what I spend on flowers every year and wonder if I'm crazy. But they have become an integral part of the dining experience at Hali'imaile. In addition to enjoying the food, our customers look forward to seeing "the new Masako." This talented artist lives in Huelo with her husband, Greg, where they grow all their own flowers and foliage. ✿

Smoked Salmon Bundles with Spicy Shrimp and Lomilomi Tomato Salsa

I made this dish up a long time ago, and it eventually found its way onto Hawaiian Airlines' first-class menu. I added a little Hawaiian flavor with the lomilomi *tomato salsa. Lomi* in Hawaiian means *"to massage or knead," and that's how you make this salsa.*

SAUCE

1/2 cup heavy cream
1/2 cup sour cream
1/4 cup good-quality mayonnaise
2 tablespoons wasabi paste
2 tablespoons Dijon mustard
1 teaspoon sugar

COURT BOUILLON

2 quarts water
1 cup dry white wine
6 black peppercorns
1 lemon, quartered
1 small onion, chopped
1 carrot, chopped
1 bouquet garni (see note)

SALMON BUNDLES

1 pound shrimp in the shell
1/2 cup good-quality mayonnaise
1/3 cup chopped fresh cilantro
1 tablespoon Vietnamese garlic-chile sauce
1 teaspoon Asian sesame oil
16 slices smoked salmon (about 14 ounces total)

LOMILOMI TOMATO SALSA

1 cup peeled, seeded, and finely diced tomato
1/4 cup finely chopped Maui onion
1/4 cup peeled, seeded, and finely diced cucumber
1 tablespoon freshly squeezed lemon juice
1 1/2 ounces salmon caviar

To prepare the sauce, in a bowl, mix together all of the ingredients until well combined. Cover and refrigerate until ready to use. (The sauce can be prepared 1 day ahead.)

To prepare the bouillon, in a saucepan, combine all the ingredients over medium-high heat. Simmer for 15 minutes.

To prepare the salmon bundles, add the shrimp to the simmering bouillon and cook for 3 minutes, until they turn pink and start to curl. Remove the shrimp from the bouillon with tongs. (The bouillon can be strained and frozen for later use, or discarded.) Peel, devein, and chop the shrimp coarsely. Place in a bowl, cover, and chill in the refrigerator for 10 minutes. Remove from the refrigerator and add the mayonnaise, cilantro, chile sauce, and sesame oil.

Arrange 2 salmon slices, overlapping slightly, on a plate. Spoon one-eighth of the shrimp mixture into the center of the salmon. Fold the salmon around the shrimp mixture, forming a bundle. Repeat with the remaining salmon slices and shrimp mixture, forming a total of 8 bundles. Cover and refrigerate until ready to use.

To prepare the salsa, in a bowl, combine the tomato, onion, cucumber, and lemon juice. Mix well. Fold in the caviar.

To assemble the dish, spoon about 3 tablespoons of the sauce onto each plate. Place a salmon bundle in the center of each plate. Divide the salsa among the plates and serve.

SERVES 8

A BOUQUET GARNI is a combination of herbs tied in a bundle or wrapped in cheesecloth, used to flavor liquids. A classic combination is 2 sprigs parsley, 6 sprigs thyme, and 1 bay leaf. It is always removed before serving.

HAMACHI WITH SIZZLING OIL,
SEAWEED SALAD, AND PONZU SAUCE

This is my favorite almost-raw fish dish. All the ingredients are just ornaments to adorn one of the most succulent fishes available. Even non-sashimi lovers will enjoy it.

PONZU SAUCE

1 tablespoon freshly squeezed lemon juice

1/4 cup soy sauce

1 teaspoon rice vinegar

1 pound very fresh hamachi (yellowtail)

1/2 cup olive oil

*3 tablespoons sesame seeds, toasted and coarsely
    ground (page 63)*

1 cup ocean seaweed salad

To make the ponzu sauce, combine all the ingredients in a bowl and mix well.

Slice the hamachi very thin and arrange in a circle on each plate. Pour spoonfuls of the ponzu sauce over the fish. In a small saucepan, heat the oil over high heat until smoking hot. Be careful not to burn the oil. Pour spoonfuls of the hot oil over the fish. Sprinkle the sesame seeds over the fish. Garnish the center of each plate with seaweed salad. Serve immediately.

SERVES 8

🍃 Even we use store-bought seaweed salad. Supermarkets here call it "ocean salad" and sell it in their fish or deli department. It is made with seaweed, agar (a Japanese gelatin), sesame seeds, vinegar, and chile peppers. Various producers flavor the salad differently. Try them all and pick your favorite. If you can't find it, a crispy cucumber salad will work fine.

SEAFOOD MARTINI WITH WASABI-GINGER COCKTAIL SAUCE

In the last five years, chefs have acquired an "anything goes" attitude toward food presentation. The martini glass, for example, has moved from the bar to the kitchen and now holds more than just vodka and an olive. It creates a great look for our cold seafood appetizer.

WASABI-GINGER COCKTAIL SAUCE

2 cups ketchup

2 tablespoons chopped pickled ginger

2 teaspoons Sriracha (Thai garlic-chile paste)

1 tablespoon fish sauce

1 tablespoon finely chopped fresh cilantro

1 cup crème fraîche (page 60)

2 tablespoons freshly squeezed lemon juice

2 cups finely shredded won bok (Chinese cabbage)

1/4 cup peeled and finely shredded carrot

1/4 cup chopped water chestnut

2 tablespoons chopped fresh cilantro

1 tablespoon chopped fresh chives

1/2 teaspoon salt

1/4 teaspoon white pepper

3 cups assorted cooked shellfish such as shrimp, lobster, crab, and scallops

6 thin lemon slices, for garnish

To prepare the sauce, in a bowl, combine all the ingredients and mix well.

In a small bowl, combine the crème fraîche with the lemon juice and stir to mix. In a bowl, toss together the cabbage, carrot, water chestnut, cilantro, and chives. Add the lemon crème fraîche, salt, and pepper and toss well.

To assemble each martini, place one-sixth of the slaw in the bottom of a chilled martini glass. Place 1/2 cup of the mixed seafood over the slaw. Top the seafood with 1 heaping tablespoon of the cocktail sauce. Garnish with a lemon slice. Serve at once.

SERVES 6

The cocktail sauce should be stored in an airtight container in the refrigerator. It will keep for up to 3 weeks. You can also use the extra on crab cakes, shrimp cocktail, fried fish, and fish cakes.

Terrine of Kula Vegetables with Roasted Tomato Vinaigrette

Once when catering a corporate party, I had to include a cooking demonstration on how to make the first course before it was served. Most people think terrines are difficult, so I showed the audience this one, to illustrate how easy and impressive they can be. We get most of our fresh produce from the farmers in the Kula area on the slopes of Mount Haleakalā. Kula is considered to have almost perfect growing conditions. Just the right amount of full sun and cloudiness at its three-thousand foot elevation, along with the rich soil, helps farmers produce wonderful locally grown vegetables and fruits.

TERRINE

1 1/2 cups chicken stock (see page 10)

2 envelopes unflavored gelatin

1 bunch cilantro, chopped

Olive oil, for sautéing

2 zucchini, thinly sliced lengthwise

3 cloves garlic, chopped

Salt

Freshly ground black pepper

1 globe eggplant, thinly sliced lengthwise

2 yellow squashes, thinly sliced lengthwise

6 mushrooms, quartered

4 tomatoes, peeled, seeded, and coarsely chopped

2 roasted red bell peppers, halved (page 97)

2 artichoke hearts, cooked and quartered (page 183)

ROASTED TOMATO VINAIGRETTE

2 large, very ripe tomatoes

Extra virgin olive oil for rubbing, plus 3/4 cup

2 cloves roasted garlic (see note)

1 tablespoon tomato paste

3 tablespoons red wine vinegar

Salt

Freshly ground black pepper

Chopped green onion, green part only, for garnish

To prepare the terrine, in a saucepan, heat the chicken stock until just hot. Add the gelatin and stir. Add half of the cilantro. Remove from the heat, cover, and set aside.

Place 2 tablespoons of the olive oil in a large skillet or sauté pan and place over medium heat. Add the zucchini, a pinch of garlic, some of the remaining cilantro, and salt and pepper to taste and sauté for 3 to 4 minutes, until just tender. Repeat with the eggplant, yellow squashes, mushrooms, and tomatoes using the remaining garlic and cilantro and increasing the oil as needed for the eggplant. The timing will vary according to the vegetable, but all should be cooked until just tender.

Line an 8 1/2 by 4 1/2-inch ceramic terrine mold with plastic wrap, leaving some extra wrap overlapping the edges. Beginning with the red peppers, layer the vegetables in the terrine, alternating them for color and texture. Reserve the mushrooms and artichokes for the middle of the terrine. In between each layer of vegetables, pour some of the stock mixture to immerse the vegetables. (If the gelatin has solidified, heat the mixture until it becomes liquid.) Finish the terrine with a layer of bell pepper and pour any remaining liquid over the top. Cover the terrine with the overhanging plastic, and weight with a full 16 1/2-ounce can to compress the vegetables. Refrigerate for at least 8 hours or up to 24 hours before slicing.

To prepare the vinaigrette, preheat the oven to 500°. Cut the tomatoes in half and squeeze out the seeds. Rub with a bit of olive oil. Place on a baking sheet and cook for about 15 minutes, until they begin to shrivel.

In a blender, combine the garlic, tomatoes, tomato paste, and vinegar and process until puréed. With the motor running, slowly add the 3/4 cup olive oil. Season to taste with salt and pepper.

To serve, invert the terrine on a plate, lift off the mold, and peel off the plastic. Slice the terrine into 10 equal portions and place on individual plates. Spoon the tomato vinaigrette over the slices and garnish with green onions.

SERVES 10

🌿 To ROAST GARLIC, first preheat the oven to 400°. Peel a whole head of garlic and place the cloves on a piece of aluminum foil. Drizzle olive oil over the garlic to coat well. Wrap the foil up into a bundle and place it in a pie tin. Place the tin in the oven and roast for 12 to 15 minutes, until the garlic is soft but not mushy. Remove from the oven and use as needed. Roasted garlic can be stored in a jar in the refrigerator for 3 to 4 days.

CURRIED SQUASH SOUP

This is one of the first soups I ever made. I used to serve it at a lot of "ladies' luncheons" in Dallas, and to my great surprise, it's one of Joe's favorite soups. It is delicious served cold, too: After puréeing, chill the soup instead of returning it to the pan. Omit the half-and-half and add 1 cup sour cream to the chilled squash mixture, then add the salt, pepper, and chives.

2 tablespoons unsalted butter

2 onions, thinly sliced

2 shallots, minced

2 pounds yellow crookneck squashes, cut into
    1-inch slices

6 cups rich chicken stock (see note)

1 cup half-and-half

1 tablespoon yellow curry powder

1 teaspoon salt

1/2 teaspoon white pepper

2 tablespoons chopped fresh chives, for garnish

In a saucepan, melt the butter over medium heat. Add the onions and shallots and cook for 4 to 5 minutes, until softened but not browned. Add the squashes and chicken stock and bring to a boil, then decrease the heat to low and simmer for 20 minutes, until the squashes are tender. Remove from the heat and strain the soup, capturing the liquid.

Place the solids in a food processor and purée in batches. Add the reserved liquid as needed to achieve a smooth consistency. Return the remaining liquid and the purée to the saucepan and add the half-and-half, curry powder, and salt and pepper to taste. Ladle into individual soup bowls and garnish with the chives.

SERVES 6

✍ I know that many home cooks simply don't have the time (or the inclination) to make their own STOCKS. Do realize, however, that homemade stocks add substantial flavor that can't be duplicated by store bought ones. If you must purchase your stock, please don't use regular old canned varieties. Meat and fish counters at most gourmet supermarkets produce quite good ones that will help your food taste just right.

Maui Onion and Ginger Soup

Our old friend Shep Gordon mastered this soup. For years, whenever he entertained at his home, guests were always greeted with a cup of this wonderful soup. As a tribute to our friendship, we put it on the menu when we opened Hali'imaile.

6 tablespoons unsalted butter

8 Maui onions, thinly sliced

1/4 cup peeled and chopped fresh ginger

8 cups rich chicken stock (see page 10)

1 cup dry white wine

8 sprigs thyme

1 cup half-and-half

1/2 teaspoon salt

1/2 teaspoon freshly ground black pepper

In a large stockpot or soup kettle, melt the butter over medium heat. Add the onions and ginger, decrease the heat to medium-low, and cook, stirring often, for about 20 minutes, until the onions are translucent. Do not allow the onions to brown, or the soup will become bitter and dark. Add the stock, wine, and thyme, increase the heat to high, and bring to a boil. Decrease the heat to low, cover partially, and cook for about 1 hour, until the onions are completely soft and falling apart.

Remove the thyme sprigs and discard. Working in batches, purée the soup in a food processor or pass it through a food mill. Return the purée to the pot and add the half-and-half, salt, and pepper. Place over medium heat and heat and stir for about 1 minute longer, until heated through. Ladle into warmed bowls and serve immediately.

SERVES 8

CARROT-GINGER SOUP
HGS CLASSIC

This is another recipe from my Dallas catering days, and it tastes much richer than it is. It's become a Hali'imaile classic over the years, and customers always smile when their servers tell them it's the soup of the day.

4 tablespoons unsalted butter

2 cups chopped onion

1/4 cup peeled and coarsely chopped fresh ginger

8 cups rich chicken stock (see page 10)

*2 pounds carrots, peeled and cut into
    1/2-inch pieces*

1 teaspoon salt

1/2 teaspoon white pepper

In a heavy saucepan, melt the butter over low heat. Add the onion and sauté for 8 to 10 minutes, until translucent. Add the ginger and cook for 5 minutes, until softened. Add the chicken stock and the carrots, increase the heat to high, and bring to a boil. Decrease the heat to medium, cover, and simmer for 25 to 30 minutes, until the carrots are fork tender.

Remove from the heat and strain the soup, capturing the liquid. Place the solids in a food processor and purée in batches. Add the reserved liquid as needed to achieve a smooth consistency. Return the remaining liquid and the purée to the saucepan.

Place over medium-low heat, season with the salt and white pepper, and heat through. Ladle into warmed bowls and serve immediately.

SERVES 8

✍ Make sure the fresh gingerroot you buy in your local market is very fresh. Look for firm, smooth, large root bulbs.

ASIAN PEAR AND DUCK TOSTADA

This dish evolved out of having to do pretty small plates for special culinary events. Everyone always does fish. So I always do duck or quail! If you can't find Asian pears, Bosc pears will do.

1 (5-pound) duck
1 tablespoon duck spice mix (page 174)
8 (6-inch) flour tortillas (page 72)

GINGER-CHILE CREAM DRESSING

1 egg yolk
1 tablespoon peeled and chopped fresh ginger
2 teaspoons soy sauce
2 teaspoons rice vinegar
$^1/_2$ teaspoon Asian sesame oil
$^1/_4$ cup honey
$^1/_2$ teaspoon salt
2 teaspoons Dijon mustard
1 teaspoon Sriracha (Thai garlic-chile paste)
2 teaspoons freshly squeezed lemon juice
$^3/_4$ cup canola oil

$^3/_4$ pound mixed baby salad greens
$^1/_2$ cup peeled and finely shredded carrot
$^1/_4$ cup sliced green onion, white part only
$^1/_4$ cup dried cranberries
2 tablespoons macadamia nut pieces, toasted
   (page 106)
2 tablespoons hoisin sauce
2 Asian pears, halved, cored, and thinly sliced
   lengthwise
$^1/_2$ cup wonton chips (page 63)

To prepare the duck, preheat the oven to 400°. Prick the skin of the duck all over with the point of a very sharp knife. Rub the duck with the spice mixture. Place in a roasting pan and roast for 20 minutes. Decrease the temperature to 350° and cook for another 40 minutes, until the juices run clear when a thigh is pierced. Transfer the duck to a platter, reserving the duck fat in the pan.

When the duck cools, remove the skin and the meat and julienne both. Place the skin in a small sauté pan. Add 2 tablespoons of the reserved duck drippings and sauté slowly over low heat. Cook for about 15 minutes, until the fat is rendered from the skin and the skin is crispy. Transfer to paper towels to drain.

Wrap the tortillas in aluminum foil and place in the oven for 6 minutes, until hot.

To prepare the dressing, place all the ingredients except the canola oil in a blender. Blend for 1 minute. With the motor running, slowly add the canola oil. If the dressing is too thick, add a small amount of water to thin it to desired consistency.

To prepare the salad, in a large bowl, mix the greens, carrot, green onion, cranberries, and macadamia nuts. Drizzle with $^3/_4$ cup of the dressing and toss to coat.

To assemble the dish, place a tortilla in the center of each plate. Brush with the hoisin sauce. Fan the pear slices on the tortillas. Divide the dressed greens among the tortillas and mound in the center. Divide the duck meat among the salads. Top with the wonton strips and duck skin cracklings and serve.

SERVES 8

SOBA NOODLE SALAD
WITH PASSION FRUIT VINAIGRETTE

This has really become a standard salad for our catering buffets. It incorporates starch with salad in one dish, and the dressing is cool and refreshing. If you can't find soba noodles, spaghetti will do. And if you can't find passion fruit, substitute concentrated frozen orange juice.

PASSION FRUIT VINAIGRETTE

5 tablespoons passion fruit purée (see note)

1 clove garlic, minced

$^1/_2$ teaspoons Dijon mustard

2 teaspoons sugar

1 teaspoon freshly squeezed lemon juice

$^3/_4$ cup olive oil

$^1/_2$ pound soba noodles

1 teaspoon Asian sesame oil

$^1/_2$ pound mixed baby salad greens

$^1/_4$ cup julienned red bell peppers

$^1/_4$ cup peeled and julienned carrots

$^1/_4$ cup julienned snow peas

2 tablespoons sliced pickled ginger

1 tablespoon sesame seeds, toasted (page 63)

2 tablespoons chopped green onions, green part only

2 tablespoons chopped fresh cilantro

2 tablespoons chopped fresh mint, plus 1 sprig for garnish

To prepare the vinaigrette, in a blender, combine all the ingredients and process until well blended. Set aside.

Bring a large pot of salted water to a boil. Add the soba noodles, stir well, and cook for 6 to 7 minutes, until al dente. Drain and rinse with cool water. Cut the noodles with scissors to achieve shorter lengths. Place in a bowl, add the sesame oil, and toss well. In a separate bowl, toss the greens with the vinaigrette.

In a large, nice glass bowl, arrange a layer of one-third of the greens. Top with a layer of one-third of the noodles. Sprinkle the noodles with one-third each of the bell pepper, carrot, snow peas, ginger, sesame seeds, green onion, cilantro, and mint. Repeat to make 2 additional layers of greens, noodles, vegetables, and seasonings.

Garnish with the sprig of mint and serve with salad tongs to include all the layers in each serving.

SERVES 4

🍃 To make your own FRESH FRUIT PURÉE, in a food processor or blender, combine 1 pound of your fruit (be it pineapple, mango, papaya, passion fruit, guava, and so on) with 1 cup simple syrup (page 44) and purée until smooth. Pass through a fine-mesh sieve to remove any fibrous tidbits, and keep refrigerated until ready to use. Fruit purées will keep in the fridge for up to 1 week. If you're looking to buy a fruit purée, most health food and gourmet markets now carry a couple frozen varieties.

Niçoise Salad with a Toss

HGS Classic

Joe's favorite salad is the French salade niçoise, which he usually enjoys with a glass of crisp Caymus Sauvignon Blanc. And, of course, because I am here in Hawai'i, I use the fresh catch of the day instead of canned tuna. I learned the thin egg strips from Roger Verge, a world-renowned chef with a two-Michelin-star restaurant in the south of France called Moulin du Mougins. He is considered one of the fathers of French cooking. Over the years, I have had the honor of spending time in the kitchen with him. Any firm fish that cooks well on the grill tastes great on top of this salad.

4 Yukon Gold potatoes, peeled
2 tablespoons shelled soybeans

OMELET CREPES
3 eggs
2 tablespoons milk
1 tablespoon unsalted butter
1 tablespoon finely chopped fresh chives
1 tablespoon finely chopped fresh flat-leaf parsley

6 (5-ounce) ahi (yellowfin) fillets

6 ounces mixed salad greens
2 ounces arugula
1 cup yellow pear tomatoes, halved lengthwise
1 cup red pear tomatoes, halved lengthwise
1/3 cup thinly sliced celery, cut on the diagonal
1/4 cup chopped green onion, white part only
1 red bell pepper, seeded and julienned
Extra virgin olive oil, for drizzling
White balsamic vinegar, for drizzling
Salt
Freshly cracked black pepper

To prepare the potatoes, fill a saucepan 3/4 full of water and bring to a boil over high heat. Add the whole potatoes and boil for 10 minutes, until cooked through but not falling apart. Drain and allow to cool. Cut into 1/4-inch slices and set aside.

To prepare the soybeans, bring a saucepan of salted water to a boil over high heat. Drop the soybeans into the water and cook for 2 to 3 minutes, until cooked but still firm. Remove with a wire skimmer and set aside to cool.

To prepare the crepe, in a bowl, beat the eggs until blended, then mix in the milk. In a nonstick omelet pan or skillet, melt the butter over medium-high heat. Pour enough of the beaten egg into the pan to cover the bottom thinly. Sprinkle with some of the chives and parsley and cook for 1 to 2 minutes, until the edges lift away from the pan. Carefully flip the crepe and cook on the second side for 1 minute, until the egg is set. Transfer to a plate. Repeat until all the egg is used.

Prepare a fire in a charcoal grill, or preheat a gas grill.

Working with 1 crepe at a time, roll up and cut crosswise into 1/2-inch slices. Shake loose and set aside.

Place the fish fillets on the grill rack and grill, turning once, for 1 1/2 to 2 minutes on each side for medium rare. Remove from the grill and keep warm.

To assemble the dish, in a large bowl, toss together the greens, arugula, tomatoes, celery, green onion, bell pepper, potato, soybeans, and egg strips. Drizzle with olive oil to coat lightly and toss, then drizzle with balsamic vinegar to coat lightly, and toss again. Season with salt and cracked pepper. Divide among 6 plates. Top each salad with a piece of grilled ahi.

SERVES 6

Rock Shrimp and Crab Cakes
with Baby Spinach and Mango Mayonnaise

This dish started out as a Sunday brunch item and has been on our lunch menu for several years. It's a solid seller—one of those workhorse dishes everyone needs in their repertoire. Crispy onion rings make a great garnish.

MANGO MAYONNAISE

1 cup finely chopped mango

3 tablespoons finely chopped green onion, white and green parts

3 tablespoons finely chopped yellow bell pepper

1 teaspoon Vietnamese garlic-chile sauce

2 tablespoons chopped mint

1/2 cup good-quality mayonnaise

Salt

2 cups cooked crabmeat

2 cups cooked, peeled, deveined, and chopped rock shrimp

2 tablespoons chopped fresh cilantro

1 tablespoon chopped fresh basil

1 tablespoon chopped red onion

1 teaspoon salt

1/2 teaspoon freshly ground black pepper

1/3 cup good-quality mayonnaise

1 1/2 cups panko (Japanese bread crumbs)

2 eggs

Peanut oil, for frying

8 cups baby spinach

To prepare the mayonnaise, in a bowl, combine all the ingredients and mix well. Set aside.

To make the cakes, first squeeze any excess liquid from the crab and shrimp. In a bowl, combine the crab, shrimp, cilantro, basil, onion, salt, and pepper. Mix well, then add the mayonnaise, 1 cup of the panko, and the eggs and stir until the mixture holds together. Divide into 8 equal portions and form each portion into a cake 1/2 inch thick and 3 inches in diameter. Coat the cakes with the remaining panko.

In a heavy sauté pan, pour in the oil to a depth of 1/4 inch and heat over medium-high heat. Working in batches, fry the cakes, turning once, for about 3 minutes on each side, until golden brown. Using a slotted spatula, transfer to paper towels to drain. Keep warm.

To assemble, place 1 cup of spinach on each plate. Top with a cake. Place 3 dollops of the mango mayonnaise on each plate. Serve at once.

SERVES 8

🌿 Japanese bread crumbs are called panko—they look like they've been shredded rather than crumbled. We use them often for their unique crunch. Look for them in Asian markets or in the Japanese food section of well-stocked supermarkets.

COULIBIAC OF OPAKAPAKA
WITH PASSION FRUIT HOLLANDAISE

My Hawaiian-flavored version of this Russian-turned-French classic. Do you think any old czars or monarchs are turning over in their graves? You can substitute salmon, halibut, or sole for the opakapaka.

2 (9$^1/_2$ by 15-inch) sheets frozen puff pastry

1 (2-pound) opakapaka fillet

2 tablespoons chopped fresh thyme

2 tablespoons chopped fresh basil

2 tablespoons chopped fresh chives

Salt

Freshly ground black pepper

2 tablespoons unsalted butter

2 shallots, minced

8 cups spinach, stems removed

6 chive crepes (page 100)

2 egg yolks beaten with 1 tablespoon water,
    for egg wash

DUXELLES

2 tablespoons unsalted butter

2 shallots, finely chopped

1 pound mushrooms, finely chopped

Salt

PASSION FRUIT HOLLANDAISE

$^1/_4$ cup rice vinegar

$^1/_2$ shallot, peeled and chopped

1 teaspoon finely chopped lemongrass,
    white part only

3 egg yolks

$^1/_8$ teaspoon cayenne pepper

2 tablespoons passion fruit purée (page 15)

1 cup unsalted butter, melted

Salt

Place the puff pastry in the refrigerator to thaw overnight.

Season both sides of the fish fillet with the thyme, basil, chives, and salt and pepper to taste.

In a sauté pan, melt the butter over medium heat. Add the shallots and then the spinach, and cook, stirring, for about 3 minutes, until just wilted. Allow to cool and then squeeze the moisture out of the spinach.

To prepare the duxelles, in a heavy sauté pan, melt the butter over low heat. Add the shallots and mushrooms, and cook, stirring occasionally, for about 5 minutes, until the liquid evaporates. Season with salt. Set aside to cool.

To assemble, place 1 sheet of the puff pastry on a clean work surface. Overlap the crepes down the center of the pastry. Spread the spinach down the center. Lay the fish fillet on the spinach. Cover the top of the fillet with the duxelles mixture. Top the fish with the second piece of pastry, cut away the excess pastry, and crimp the edges together to seal. Cut the excess pastry into strips to use as a crisscross design for the top of the coulibiac. Brush the coulibiac with the egg wash. Top with the cut-out pastry pieces, the egg wash will adhere them. Place the coulibiac in the refrigerator for 1 hour to chill.

Preheat the oven to 375°. Place the coulibiac in the oven and bake for 30 minutes, until the pastry is golden brown. Let sit for 10 minutes before slicing.

Meanwhile, prepare the passion fruit hollandaise: in a small saucepan, combine the vinegar, shallot, and lemongrass over medium heat. Simmer for 10 to 12 minutes, until reduced to 1 tablespoon. Strain the mixture through a fine-mesh sieve, capturing the liquid and discarding the solids. Place the reserved liquid into a blender and add the egg yolks, cayenne pepper, and passion fruit purée and process to mix. With the motor running, slowly add the butter. Season to taste with salt, and keep warm in a thermos.

To serve, slice the coulibiac into wedges and place on individual plates. Drizzle the hollandaise over the top of the wedges and around the plates.

SERVES 8

🌿 The best brand of puff pastry I've found is Pepperidge Farm, and the best phyllo is Apollo. The easiest way to keep a butter sauce warm is to place it in a coffee thermos. The thermos will hold the sauce at the correct temperature for a few hours and prevent it from breaking.

SALMON STRUDEL

For years, this was my big daytime wedding entrée, served with a simple green salad. Brides would call and say they'd had it at someone else's wedding and then wanted it for theirs.

3/4 pound salmon fillet

2 cups water

1/2 lemon, quartered

1 bay leaf

2 tablespoons unsalted butter

2 tablespoons flour

3/4 cup milk

2 tablespoons heavy cream

Salt

White pepper

1 cup panko (Japanese bread crumbs)

1/4 cup grated Asiago cheese

1 teaspoon mustard powder

8 sheets phyllo dough (about 1/2 pound)

1/2 cup clarified butter, melted (page 167)

1/4 pound smoked salmon, cut into 1/4-inch-wide strips

1/2 cup firmly packed herb and garlic cheese spread, crumbled

2 hard-boiled eggs, chopped

3/4 cup sour cream

1/4 cup chopped fresh dill

1/4 cup sliced green onion

2 tablespoons chopped fresh chives

2 tablespoons chopped fresh flat-leaf parsley

1/4 cup salmon caviar

To poach the salmon, in a saucepan, bring the water, lemon, and bay leaf to a simmer over medium heat. Add the salmon fillet and cook gently for 10 to 12 minutes, until cooked through and no longer opaque in the center. With a slotted spoon, remove the fillet and place on a plate to cool. When completely cool, use a fork to flake the salmon into 1-inch pieces.

To prepare the sauce, in a saucepan, melt the butter over medium heat until bubbling but not brown. Remove from the heat, whisk in the flour, and return to the heat for 2 minutes, stirring constantly. Pour in the milk, while stirring constantly. Add the cream and then season with salt and white pepper. Cook, stirring, for 3 to 4 minutes, until thickened. Transfer to a bowl and chill for 2 hours, until firm.

To prepare the strudel, in a bowl, combine the panko, Asiago cheese, and mustard and mix well.

Unroll the phyllo on a sheet of waxed paper. Take 1 sheet of phyllo and place with a long side facing you on a marble or a wood cutting board. Keep the remaining phyllo covered to prevent it from drying out. Brush the phyllo sheet with the clarified butter and sprinkle with the panko mixture. Repeat until you have 8 layers. On the bottom one-third of the long side closest to you, arrange the salmon and smoked salmon. Dot with the herb and garlic cheese. Sprinkle with the egg. Dot with the sour cream. In a small bowl, mix together the dill, green onion, chives, and parsley. Sprinkle over the top. Dot with the chilled sauce. Fold both short sides over the ends of the filling and then roll up jelly roll style. Chill for 20 minutes. Meanwhile, preheat the oven to 400°.

Butter a baking sheet. Place the strudel, seam side down, on the pan. Brush with the remaining clarified butter. Place in the oven and decrease the temperature to 375°. Bake for 30 minutes, until crisp and brown. Let cool for 10 minutes, then slice to serve. Top each slice with a dollop of salmon caviar.

SERVES 6

MIXED GRILL OF HAWAIIAN SNAPPER
WITH CHARDONNAY SAUCE

My "unofficial" catering in Hawai'i began by cooking for families on vacation. This dish was one of the building blocks of my reputation. People loved the sauce so much, they ate what was left on the plate with a spoon. Don't skimp on the price of the chardonnay—the better the wine, the better the sauce. Opakapaka, onaga, and uku are all types of local deepwater snapper. Pacific snapper, sea bass, and halibut can be substituted.

CHARDONNAY SAUCE

2 tablespoons olive oil

3¹/2 tablespoons unsalted butter

¹/4 cup peeled and chopped carrot

2 tablespoons chopped celery

2 tablespoons chopped onion

2 tablespoons chopped leek, white part only

1¹/2 tablespoons fresh thyme leaves

1¹/2 tablespoons fresh tarragon leaves

1¹/2 tablespoons fresh flat-leaf parsley leaves

1 tablespoon black peppercorns

1 pound fresh fish bones (no gills or blood lines)

1 (750-ml) bottle chardonnay

1¹/2 cups heavy cream

Salt

Freshly ground black pepper

3/4 pound opakapaka fillet, cut into 4 equal pieces

3/4 pound onaga fillet, cut into 4 equal pieces

3/4 pound uku fillet, cut into 4 equal pieces

¹/4 cup olive oil

Salt

Freshly ground black pepper

To prepare the sauce, in a large saucepan, melt the oil and 2 tablespoons of the butter over medium-high heat. Add the carrot, celery, onion, and leek and cook for 5 minutes, until limp. Add the thyme, tarragon, parsley, peppercorns, and fish bones and cook, stirring, for 5 minutes, until the meat on the bones turns white. Add the chardonnay, cover, and simmer for 30 minutes, until the flavors marry together.

Remove from the heat and pour through a cheesecloth-lined sieve into a clean saucepan. Place over medium heat and reduce to ¹/4 cup. Add the cream and continue to simmer for 25 minutes, until reduced to 1 cup. Swirl in the remaining 1¹/2 tablespoons butter just before serving. Season to taste with salt and pepper.

While the sauce is cooking, prepare a fire in a charcoal grill, or preheat a gas grill. When the grill is ready, brush the fish fillets with the oil and place on the grill rack. Grill, turning once, for 3 minutes on each side, or until just opaque at the center.

To serve, place 1 piece of each kind of fish on individual plates. Spoon the sauce over the top of the fish and serve at once.

SERVES 4

CRAB CANNELLONI
WITH LEMONGRASS-GINGER SAUCE

This is one of those dishes that you know you shouldn't eat but you will and not only that, you'll eat the whole rich and delicious thing. Whenever we make these at food events, after ten minutes, we have the longest lines waiting to get the cannelloni.

LEMONGRASS-GINGER SAUCE

6 cups heavy cream

1 lemongrass stalk, white part only, pounded

1 tablespoon peeled and chopped fresh ginger

Grated zest and juice of 3 limes

2 teaspoons salt

2 teaspoons white pepper

2 tablespoons unsalted butter

2 tablespoons peeled and finely chopped carrot

2 tablespoons finely chopped onion

2 cloves garlic, minced

2 shallots, minced

1 pound cooked shredded crabmeat, preferably Dungeness

1 1/2 cups ricotta cheese

1/4 cup shredded Parmesan cheese

2 tablespoons finely chopped green onion, white and green parts

2 tablespoons chopped fresh cilantro

1 tablespoon chopped fresh chives

3 eggs, beaten

1/2 teaspoon salt

1/4 teaspoon white pepper

2 tablespoons olive oil

12 (5-inch-square) fresh pasta sheets

1 tablespoon chopped fresh chives, for garnish

2 tablespoons tobiko (flying fish roe), for garnish

To prepare the sauce, in a saucepan, combine the cream, lemongrass, and ginger. Place over medium-high heat and boil gently for 45 minutes, until reduced by half. Stir in the lime zest and juice, salt, and pepper. Remove from the heat and remove and discard the lemongrass.

To prepare the cannelloni filling, in a skillet, melt the butter over medium heat. Add the carrot, onion, garlic, and shallots and sauté for 5 minutes, until the onions are translucent. Transfer to a bowl. Add the crab, ricotta, Parmesan, green onion, cilantro, and chives and stir to combine. Add the eggs, salt, and pepper and mix well.

To prepare the pasta, line 3 baking sheets with parchment paper and lightly spray with vegetable-oil cooking spray. In a large saucepan, bring salted water to a boil over high heat. Add the oil and, using a slotted spoon, add the pasta sheets a few at a time. Boil for 1 minute, until pliable but not completely cooked. Drain and allow to cool flat on the prepared baking sheets.

Preheat the oven to 350°. Evenly spread 3/4 cup of the sauce in the bottom of a 9 by 12-inch baking dish. Place about 1/4 cup of the crab mixture near the edge of a pasta sheet and roll up into a cylinder. Place seam side down in the prepared dish. Repeat with the remaining pasta sheets and filling. Cover with the remaining sauce. Bake for 20 minutes, until the sauce is bubbling. To serve, place 2 cannelloni in the center of each individual plate and garnish with the chopped chives and tobiko.

SERVES 6

🍤 Tobiko, flying fish roe, has a wonderful crunchy texture. It comes in red, green (flavored with wasabi), and gold and a small amount sprinkled on seafood dishes adds some beautiful color.

SESAME-CRUSTED MAHIMAHI
WITH COCONUT-CURRY CABBAGE
AND RUM-BAKED BANANAS

This is the epitome of Hawai'i Regional Cuisine, especially when you remember that cabbage is a big crop on the islands. During many months of the year, the bananas for this dish come from the trees in my backyard. For this recipe, as with most of my cooking, I prefer to use frozen coconut milk, but regular canned will do. A note of explanation: in 1991, twelve Island chefs, including myself, formed a coalition designed to celebrate and perpetuate the diversity and sophistication of the Islands' bounty. A unique new cuisine, Hawai'i Regional Cuisine, was born out of the collaboration between these chefs and the local farmers, who in turn became dedicated to growing a wider variety of ingredients.

COCONUT-CURRY CABBAGE

1 tablespoon canola oil

1 small onion, chopped

1 to 2 tablespoons yellow Thai curry paste

8 cups shredded green cabbage

2 cups frozen coconut milk, thawed

1/2 teaspoon fish sauce

RUM-BAKED BANANAS

1 tablespoon unsalted butter

1/4 cup firmly packed brown sugar

1/4 cup dark rum

4 large ripe bananas

2 cups panko (Japanese bread crumbs)

1/4 cup chopped fresh basil

2 cloves garlic

3 tablespoons sesame seeds, toasted (page 63)

1 cup good-quality mayonnaise

1 1/2 teaspoons sambal (Indonesian garlic-chile paste)

8 (6-ounce) mahimahi fillets

Salt

Freshly ground black pepper

Canola oil, for sautéing

To prepare the cabbage, in a large sauté pan, heat the oil over high heat. Add the onion and curry paste and sauté for 3 minutes, until the onion is softened. Add the cabbage and sauté for 1 minute longer, until limp. Add the coconut milk and simmer for 2 to 3 minutes, until the cabbage is tender. Add fish sauce to taste.

To prepare the bananas, preheat the oven to 450°. In a saucepan, melt the butter over medium-high heat. Add the brown sugar and cook, stirring occasionally, for 2 minutes, until the sugar melts. Remove from the burner and add the rum. Ignite with a long match, allow the flame to die down, and return to the burner. Simmer the mixture for about 4 minutes, until a thick syrup forms. Cut the bananas in half lengthwise and place in a baking dish with the rum syrup. Place in the oven for 2 to 3 minutes, until the bananas are soft. Remove from the oven and brush with the syrup that has collected in the bottom of the dish. Keep warm.

To make the coating, in a food processor, combine the panko, basil, garlic, and sesame seeds and process until a fine bread-crumb consistency forms. In a small bowl, mix together the mayonnaise and chile paste. Lightly season the fish fillets with salt and pepper and brush with chile mayonnaise on one side. Spread the panko mixture in a flat pan and place the fish fillets on it, mayonnaise side down. Press firmly to adhere the crumb mixture.

In a large sauté pan, pour in enough canola oil to cover the bottom of the pan and place over high heat. Add the fish fillets,

coated side down. Sauté for 2 minutes, until golden brown. Turn the fillets and sauté for 4 to 5 minutes, until cooked through.

To serve, place one-eighth of the cabbage in each individual shallow bowl. Place a fish fillet on top of each bed of cabbage. Garnish each plate with one of the banana halves.

SERVES 8

🌿 The rum-baked bananas are a wonderful side dish with curries or roast pork. They are also very good with vanilla ice cream!

SHRIMP AND SCALLOP STIR-FRY
WITH PINEAPPLE FRIED RICE

I was in the restaurant-supply store one day and saw those cute little covered stainless-steel dishes with pedestal bases used in old-fashioned Chinese restaurants. I wanted them for Hali'imaile, so I created a menu item to serve in them.

LOBSTER SAUCE

4 cups shrimp shells

2 tablespoons olive oil

1/4 cup chopped onion

1/4 cup peeled and chopped carrot

1/4 cup chopped celery

4 cloves garlic, minced

1 tablespoon lemongrass ginger pesto (page 162)

1/3 cup dry sherry

2/3 cup dry white wine

6 cups fish stock (see page 10)

1 bay leaf

1 teaspoon black peppercorns

4 to 6 sprigs thyme

1 tablespoon sugar

2 tablespoons tomato paste

1 tablespoon lobster or fish base

3 teaspoons cornstarch

3 teaspoons water

PINEAPPLE FRIED RICE

7 tablespoons peanut oil

1/2 cup peeled and finely diced pineapple

1/4 cup sliced water chestnuts

2 tablespoons peeled and finely diced carrot

2 tablespoons peeled and finely diced fresh ginger

1/4 cup thinly sliced Chinese sausage

1/4 cup diced red onion

1/4 cup green peas

3 cups cooked white rice, cooled

1/2 teaspoon salt

Pinch of freshly ground black pepper

3 tablespoons canola oil

1 cup peeled and julienned carrot

1/2 cup sliced onion

1/2 cup chopped red cabbage

1/2 cup snow peas

1/2 red bell pepper, seeded and sliced

1 cup baby bok choy

1 pound large shrimp (16 to 20), peeled and deveined, shells reserved for lobster sauce

1 pound scallops

1 cup shiitake mushrooms, stemmed and halved

Preheat the oven to 400°. To prepare the lobster sauce, place the shrimp shells in a roasting pan and roast for 10 minutes, until crispy brown. Transfer to a food processor and process to chop coarsely. In a heavy stockpot, heat the olive oil over medium-high heat. Add the onion, carrot, celery, and garlic and sauté for 2 minutes, until limp. Add the pesto and cook for 5 minutes, until the vegetables are softened. Add the shrimp shells and deglaze the pan with the sherry and white wine, stirring to dislodge any browned bits. Add the stock, bay leaf, peppercorns, thyme, sugar, tomato paste, and lobster base and stir well. Bring to a boil, then decrease the heat to low and simmer to reduce for about 30 minutes. Strain through a fine-mesh sieve and return to the saucepan. Place over medium heat and simmer until reduced by half. You should have 2 cups. In a small bowl, stir together the cornstarch and water. Add to the sauce and stir to mix well.

To prepare the fried rice, in a large sauté pan, heat the peanut oil over high heat until smoking. Add the pineapple, water chestnuts, carrot, ginger, sausage, onion, and peas and stir-fry for 3 to 5 minutes. Add the rice, salt, and pepper and

(continued)

continue to stir-fry for 3 minutes, until the rice is heated through. Spoon onto a warmed platter.

To prepare the stir-fry, in a large wok, heat the canola oil over high heat. Add the carrot, onion, and cabbage and stir-fry for 1 minute, until al dente. Add the snow peas, bell pepper, bok choy, shrimp, and scallops and stir-fry for 2 to 3 minutes, until the vegetables and seafood are just cooked. Add the mushrooms and stir-fry for 2 minutes, until softened. Add 1 cup of the lobster sauce and stir well. Add the remaining lobster sauce and simmer for 1 minute. Pour over the fried rice. Serve immediately.

SERVES 6

There's really no substitute for homemade fish stock, but if you must, you can use good-quality bottled clam juice.

ANCHO CHILE–MARINATED UKU
WITH CORN SALSA AND GINGER CREAM

Since fresh fish is the staple at every good restaurant—and home—in Hawai'i, the idea is to come up with creative things to put under, on top, and to the side of precisely cooked fish. The flavor of the fish should be enhanced, not masked. This is a perfect example. You can substitute any snapper, sole, perch, or cod for the uku.

1 ancho chile, stemmed
2 cloves garlic, minced
2 tablespoons chopped fresh cilantro
Grated zest and juice of 1 lime
2 tablespoons olive oil
6 (6-ounce) uku (gray snapper) fillets

CORN SALSA

1 tablespoon olive oil
3 cups corn kernels (from about 6 ears)
Juice of 3 limes
1 red onion, chopped
1 tomato, seeded and chopped
1 1/2 teaspoons chopped chipotle chile in adobo plus 2 teaspoons adobo sauce
Salt
Freshly ground black pepper

GINGER CREAM

1/2 cup dry white wine
1/2 cup rice vinegar
3 shallots, minced
1 tablespoon peeled and sliced fresh ginger
1 cup heavy cream
1 tablespoon passion fruit purée (page 15)
1 cup chilled butter, cut into pieces
Salt

To prepare the marinade, in a dry sauté pan, add the chile and sauté for 1 1/2 to 2 minutes, until it begins to blacken. Place in a heatproof bowl, add boiling water to cover, and let stand for 10 to 15 minutes, until softened. Drain and place the chile in a food processor with the garlic, cilantro, lime zest and juice, and olive oil. Process to form a marinade. Transfer to a nonreactive container, add the fish fillets, and marinate for 1 hour at room temperature.

To prepare the salsa, in a sauté pan, heat the olive oil over high heat. Add the corn and quickly sear for 30 seconds. Add the lime juice, sauté for 30 seconds, and remove from the heat. Transfer to a bowl and allow to cool. Add all the remaining ingredients including salt and pepper to taste, and toss well.

Prepare a fire in a charcoal grill, or preheat a gas grill.

To prepare the cream, in a saucepan, combine the wine, vinegar, shallots, and ginger and bring to a boil over high heat. Boil to reduce until the mixture is syrupy. This should take 7 to 8 minutes. Add the cream and passion fruit purée. Continue to cook for 5 minutes, until reduced by half. Strain into a clean saucepan over low heat. Whisk in the butter, a piece at a time. Season with a pinch of salt.

Remove the fish from the marinade and place on the grill rack. Grill, turning once, for 3 to 4 minutes on each side until cooked to medium.

To serve, place one-sixth of the salsa in the center of each individual plate. Place a fish fillet on top of the salsa and drizzle the cream over the fish.

SERVES 6

🌿 Chipotle chiles in adobo sauce are smoked jalapeños packed in a tomato-vinegar mixture. They are smoky and quite spicy. Add more if you like your food hot, or substitute fresh jalapeño.

ANGEL HAIR PASTA WITH
TOMATOES, BASIL, AND PINE NUTS

This is something that I made at home a lot. Joe said if we ever opened a restaurant, it had to be on the menu. It's one of those simple, but incredibly flavorful dishes. It is an absolute must to use the ripest tomatoes and the best extra virgin olive oil available. The wonderful flavor of this dish is directly linked to the quality of those two ingredients.

1¼ cups extra virgin olive oil
4 shallots, chopped
4 cloves garlic, minced
½ cup capers, drained
4 cups peeled, seeded, and chopped tomato
¾ cup finely shredded fresh basil
1½ teaspoons salt
Freshly ground black pepper
½ pound dried angel hair pasta
½ cup pine nuts, toasted (page 106)
½ cup shredded Parmesan cheese
8 basil leaves, for garnish

In a large sauté pan, heat ¼ cup of the olive oil over medium-low heat. Add the shallots and garlic and sauté for 3 minutes, until softened. Add the capers and cook for 1 minute. Add the tomato and the remaining 1 cup olive oil. Cook for about 5 minutes, until the mixture is heated through. Stir in the shredded basil and season with salt and pepper to taste.

Meanwhile, bring a large pot of water to a boil. Add the pasta and cook for 2 to 3 minutes, until al dente. Drain well and transfer to a bowl.

Pour the sauce over the pasta. Reserving 1 tablespoon each for garnish, add the pine nuts and Parmesan cheese and toss to coat evenly. Serve in individual bowls garnished with the reserved pine nuts and Parmesan and the basil leaves.

SERVES 4

🍃 The best way to seed a tomato is to cut it in half horizontally, put one-half in each hand cut side down, hold them over the sink, and squeeze. The seeds drop right out. Now, isn't that easier than the way you've been doing it?

SMOKED CHICKEN TORTELLONI
WITH A TRIO OF MUSTARD CREAM SAUCE

I made up this recipe for an annual fundraising event at the Four Seasons in Wailea. For years, participating chefs would come up with interesting pasta dishes to serve for dinner the day before the Terry Fox Run to benefit cancer research. This "carbo-loading" dinner soon turned into a "taste of Hawai'i" food event that entices over six hundred people to participate and feast on delicious dishes from local chefs. Thousands of dollars are raised each year.

1¹/2 *pounds smoked chicken meat*

¹/4 *cup grated Asiago cheese*

2 *tablespoons cornstarch*

2 *tablespoons water*

1 *(12-ounce) package 3-inch-square wonton skins*

4 *cups heavy cream*

2 *teaspoons finely chopped garlic*

1 *tablespoon finely chopped shallot*

¹/3 *cup Dijon mustard*

1 *tablespoon Maui onion mustard or honey mustard*

2 *tablespoons whole-grain mustard*

Pinch of salt

¹/4 *cup julienned fresh basil, for garnish*

1 *tomato, seeded and diced, for garnish*

Place the chicken meat and Asiago cheese in the bowl of a food processor and pulse until finely ground.

In a small bowl, stir together the cornstarch and water. To prepare the tortelloni, lay out the wonton skins and place 1 heaping teaspoon of chicken in the center of each wrapper. Brush the edges with the cornstarch mixture. Fold the edge up to form a triangle. Brush the 2 pointed edges with the cornstarch mixture, fold them in toward each other, and press to seal. Repeat until all the chicken is used. Cover, place the tortelloni in the refrigerator, and chill for at least 1 hour. (If not being used immediately, they can be stored in the freezer for up to 1 month.)

Pour the cream into a saucepan and add the garlic and shallot. Place over medium-high heat and cook until reduced and the cream thickens. This should take about 15 minutes. Add the mustards and reduce slightly. Pour through a fine mesh sieve into a clean saucepan. Keep warm.

In a saucepan, bring water to a boil over high heat. Add the salt and the tortelloni and cook for 4 minutes, until al dente. Drain and place in a bowl.

Add the sauce to the tortelloni and toss well. Garnish with the basil and tomato and serve.

SERVES 6

🖉 You can substitute wonton skins for pasta sheets when making any small filled pastas.

CRUNCHY MACADAMIA NUT CHICKEN
OVER TROPICAL FRUIT PAELLA

Once you've tasted this, you will remember it as one of the best things you've ever put in your mouth.
It's a variation on your typical fried chicken since the coating includes macadamia nuts.

TROPICAL FRUIT PAELLA

1 cup jasmine rice

1/4 cup olive oil

1 onion, diced

1 lemongrass stalk, pounded

1 teaspoon kosher salt

2 cups chicken stock (see page 10)

2 tablespoons peeled and chopped fresh ginger

1 tablespoon chopped garlic

1 large red bell pepper, seeded and diced

2 tablespoons chopped green onion, white part only

1/4 cup diced water chestnuts

1/2 cup diced lychee nuts, fresh or canned

1/2 small pineapple, peeled and diced

1 mango, pitted, peeled, and diced

1 papaya, seeded, peeled, and diced

PINEAPPLE CHUTNEY DIPPING SAUCE

1 cup mango chutney

1/2 cup diced pineapple

1/2 cup good-quality mayonnaise

1 cup quick rolled oats

1/2 cup macadamia nuts

2 tablespoons flour

1 teaspoon dried thyme

2 tablespoons grated Parmesan cheese

Salt

Freshly ground black pepper

4 (6-ounce) boneless, skinless chicken breast halves

1 cup unsalted butter, melted

1/4 cup canola oil

To prepare the paella, place the rice in a sieve and rinse under cold running water until the water runs clear. Drain well. In a saucepan, heat 2 tablespoons of the oil over medium heat. Add the onion and sauté for 3 minutes, until softened. Add the rice, lemongrass, and salt and stir well. Add the stock, stir, cover, and cook for 12 to 14 minutes over medium heat until the rice is tender and the liquid is absorbed. Remove and discard the lemongrass.

Meanwhile, in a skillet, heat the remaining 2 tablespoons oil over medium-high heat. Add the ginger and the garlic and sauté for 4 to 5 minutes, until softened. Add the bell pepper, green onion, water chestnuts, lychee nuts, and all the fruits and sauté lightly for 2 minutes, until heated through. Add this mixture to the rice and toss to combine. Keep warm until serving.

To prepare the dipping sauce, combine all the ingredients in a bowl and mix well. Set aside.

To make the coating, put the rolled oats in a food processor and pulse until finely chopped. Transfer to a bowl. Put the macadamia nuts in the food processor and pulse just until finely chopped but not stuck together. Add the nuts to the oatmeal and mix well. Add the flour, thyme, and Parmesan cheese and mix well. Season with salt and pepper.

Dip the chicken breasts in the butter. Dredge the breasts in the oats mixture until they are well coated. In a large skillet, heat the canola oil over medium-high heat. Add the chicken breasts skin side down and fry, turning once, for about 4 minutes on each side, until crispy, brown, and cooked through. Transfer to paper towels to drain.

To serve, place a spoonful of the paella in the center of each individual plate, and top with a chicken breast. Serve with the dipping sauce alongside.

SERVES 4

Piña Colada Cheesecake
HGS Classic

Here is the perfect cheesecake for Hawai'i for obvious reasons. It is perfect for our restaurant as well, since we're in the middle of a working pineapple plantation. This glorious dessert has been on the menu almost since day one, and it was on the cover of Food & Wine *magazine in March 1992, a fact upon which our servers capitalize to this day! If the restaurant has one signature dessert, this is it. — T.G.*

White Chocolate Ganache
Makes 3/4 cup

1/4 cup heavy cream
4 ounces white chocolate, chopped

Graham Cracker Crust

2 cups graham cracker crumbs
1 cup shredded dried coconut
1/4 cup granulated sugar
7 tablespoons unsalted butter, melted

Sautéed Pineapple

1 tablespoon unsalted butter
1/4 large pineapple, peeled and chopped
1/4 cup firmly packed brown sugar

Cheesecake Mix

1 pound cream cheese, at room temperature
1 cup granulated sugar
1/3 cup sour cream
2 tablespoons cream of coconut, preferably Coco Lopez
2 eggs

16 Pineapple Shortbread Cookies (page 134), for decoration
2 tablespoons shredded dried coconut, for decoration

To prepare the ganache, in a saucepan, bring the cream to a boil over medium-high heat. Remove from the heat and stir in the chocolate until melted. Allow to cool, cover, and refrigerate overnight. Bring to room temperature before using.

To prepare the crust, in a bowl, mix together the crumbs, coconut, and sugar. Pour in the butter and toss to mix. Spray a 10-inch fluted tart pan with a removable bottom with vegetable-oil cooking spray. Press the mixture into the bottom and sides of the prepared pan.

Preheat the oven to 300°. To prepare the pineapple, in a skillet, melt the butter over medium-high heat. Add the pineapple and brown sugar and sauté for 10 minutes, until caramelized. Remove from the heat, drain through a sieve, and set aside.

To prepare the cheesecake mix, in a bowl, using an electric mixer on medium speed, beat the cream cheese until smooth. Slowly add the sugar, then the sour cream and cream of coconut while continuing to beat. Scrape down the sides of the bowl and add the eggs, one at a time, beating well after each addition.

To assemble the cake, spoon the pineapple onto the crust in an even layer. Pour the cream cheese mixture onto the pineapple layer. Bake for 1 hour. Turn the oven off and let the cheesecake sit in the oven for 1 1/2 hours longer. Remove from the oven and allow to cool. Cover and refrigerate for 4 to 6 hours.

Unmold by removing the pan sides and sliding the cake onto a serving plate. Spoon the ganache into a pastry bag fitted with a 2-inch star tip, and pipe 8 rosettes decoratively on the top. Lean 2 cookies vertically against each rosette and sprinkle the top of the cake with the coconut.

Serves 8

LILIKOʻI, GUAVA, AND WHITE CHOCOLATE CHEESECAKE

There's only so much Piña Colada Cheesecake one can make, so I started making this cake to add some diversity to the pastry chef's (my!) routine. It's my sister Jana's favorite, so for a birthday surprise one year, I sent her one in Los Angeles. Lots of dry ice and bubble wrap! — *T.G.*

¹/₂ cup white chocolate ganache (page 37)

WHITE CHOCOLATE GRAHAM CRACKER CRUST

2 cups graham cracker crumbs
¹/₄ cup sugar
2 ounces white chocolate, finely chopped
7 tablespoons unsalted butter, melted

FILLING I

1 pound cream cheese, at room temperature
1 cup sugar
¹/₃ cup sour cream
¹/₄ cup likoʻi purée or passion fruit purée (page 15)
2 eggs

FILLING II

¹/₂ pound cream cheese, at room temperature
¹/₂ cup sugar
3 tablespoons sour cream
¹/₄ cup guava purée (page 15)
1 egg

Prepare the ganache as directed and refrigerate overnight.

To prepare the crust, in a bowl, mix together the crumbs, sugar, and chocolate. Pour in the butter and toss to mix. Spray a 10-inch fluted tart pan with a removable bottom with vegetable-oil cooking spray. Press the mixture into the bottom and sides of the prepared pan.

Preheat the oven to 300°.

To prepare filling I, in a bowl, using an electric mixer on medium speed, cream together the cream cheese and sugar until fluffy. Add the sour cream and beat to combine. Beat in the likoʻi purée. Scrape down the sides of the bowl and add the eggs, one at a time, beating well after each addition.

To prepare filling II, in a bowl, using an electric mixer on medium speed, cream together the cream cheese and sugar until fluffy. Add the sour cream and beat to combine. Beat in the guava purée. Scrape down the sides of the bowl. Add the egg and beat well.

To assemble the cake, pour the likoʻi mixture into the crust, then spoon in the guava mixture and swirl with a knife. Bake for 1 hour. Turn off the oven and let the cheesecake sit in the oven for 1¹/₂ hours longer. Remove from the oven and allow to cool. Cover and refrigerate for 4 to 6 hours. Unmold by removing the pan sides and sliding the cake onto a serving plate. Spoon the ganache into a pastry bag fitted with a 2-inch star tip, and pipe rosettes decoratively on the top.

SERVES 6 TO 8

🌿 Likoʻi is a fruit grown on trees in Hawaiʻi. It resembles a round lemon with smooth skin. When you cut the fruit open, it is filled with almost bitter pomegranate-like seeds. The seeds are puréed and strained for use in cooking. If making your own purée, be sure not to overpurée, or the fruit becomes bitter. I get my likoʻi purée from a sweet local lady who grows the fruit in Hāʻiku, but frozen guava and passion fruit purées are more widely available and work just fine.

Guava-Raspberry Crème Brûlée

One of my various "takes" on crème brûlée using local fruits for tropical flavor. I slow-bake mine: it doesn't soufflé or bubble, it's just super creamy. I use no milk, only cream. — T.G.

Guava Filling

1/4 cup guava purée (page 15)
1/2 cup simple syrup (page 44)
2 tablespoons cornstarch
1 tablespoon water
24 fresh raspberries

Crème Brûlée Mix

3 cups heavy cream
3/4 cup granulated sugar
1 tablespoon peeled and minced fresh ginger
1/2 vanilla bean, split lengthwise
8 egg yolks

1/2 cup raw sugar

To prepare the filling, in a saucepan, bring the guava purée and simple syrup to a boil over low heat. Meanwhile, in a small bowl, stir together the cornstarch and water. When the purée is boiling, whisk in the cornstarch mixture and continue cooking and whisking until mixture comes to a rapid boil. Turn off the heat and let cool slightly.

Place 6 of the raspberries in each of 4 (1-cup) custard cups. Spoon the guava filling on top of the raspberries and press down with a spoon so the mixture will stick to the berries and the filling will stick to the bottom of the cup. Cover and refrigerate, preferably overnight.

To prepare the crème brûlée mix, in a saucepan, combine the cream, granulated sugar, and ginger over medium heat. Using the tip of a sharp knife, scrape the seeds from the vanilla bean into the pan, then add the pod. Bring to a boil. Meanwhile, in a bowl, using a wire whisk, beat the egg yolks until blended. When the cream mixture is boiling, slowly pour it into the egg yolks while whisking constantly. Pour through a fine-mesh sieve into a clean bowl. Allow to cool, then cover and refrigerate for at least 2 hours or up to overnight.

Preheat the oven to 300°. Place the custard cups in a high-sided baking pan. Fill each cup almost to the top with the crème brûlée mix. Fill the pan with hot water to reach about halfway up the sides of the cups. Carefully place in the oven and bake for 1 1/2 hours, until the custard is firm and turns dark yellow. Remove from the oven and let cool in the water bath, then remove from the water bath, cover, and refrigerate for several hours before serving. When ready to serve, spread the top of each custard with 2 tablespoons of the raw sugar. Using a butane torch, caramelize the sugar. Alternatively, place the cups on a baking sheet and slip under a hot broiler just long enough to caramelize the sugar. Watch closely as they burn easily. Serve immediately.

Serves 4

🍃 I make my crème brûlée mix the day before, so the berries don't float to the top when I pour it over them.

DOUBLE COCONUT CREAM CAKE

The pastry chef at Mustards, in Napa, California, gave me this recipe to make for a friend of hers who was getting married on Maui. After making it for the wedding, I realized what an excellent cake it is for Hawai'i. We had never had a great coconut cake before. So I added some of my own touches, and it's been a hit ever since. — T.G.

COCONUT CAKE

3¹/2 cups sifted cake flour

1 tablespoon plus 2 teaspoons baking powder

2 teaspoons salt

¹/2 teaspoon ground nutmeg

³/4 cup unsalted butter, at room temperature

Seeds from 1 vanilla bean

2¹/3 cups sugar

1¹/2 cups frozen coconut milk, thawed

2 cups shredded dried coconut, toasted

8 egg whites

1 cup cream of coconut, preferably Coco Lopez

2 cups pastry cream (page 184)

BUTTERCREAM FROSTING
MAKES 6 CUPS

1 cup egg whites (about 8)

2 cups sugar

6 tablespoons water

2 cups (1 pound) unsalted butter, at room temperature

¹/4 cup water

Toasted, shredded dried coconut for decorating

Preheat the oven to 325°. Butter the bottom and sides of a 10-inch cake pan, line the bottom with parchment paper, then butter and flour the paper and flour the sides.

To prepare the cake, in a bowl, sift together the flour, baking powder, salt, and nutmeg. In another bowl, using an electric mixer on medium speed, cream together the butter, vanilla seeds, and 2 cups of the sugar until fluffy. Reduce the speed to low and add the flour mixture in 3 batches, alternating with the coconut milk and beginning and ending with the flour mixture. Transfer to a larger bowl and fold in the coconut.

In a clean bowl, using the mixer on medium speed with clean beaters, whip the egg whites until foamy. Add the remaining ¹/3 cup sugar and whip until soft peaks form. Fold the whites into the batter in 2 additions.

Pour the batter into the prepared pan and bake for 40 to 50 minutes, until golden brown. Allow to cool on a rack, then turn the cake out of the pan and peel off the parchment. Using a serrated knife, cut horizontally into 3 layers.

Meanwhile, add ¹/2 cup of the cream of coconut to the pastry cream and mix well. Reserve the remaining cream of coconut for soaking the cake.

Be sure to have a candy thermometer to prepare the buttercream. Put the egg whites in a clean bowl. Combine the sugar and water in a small saucepan over medium-high heat and bring to a boil. As soon as the mixture begins to boil, start to beat the egg whites with an electric mixer on low speed. Beat until soft peaks form. When the sugar mixture reaches 240°, remove from the heat. If you don't have a candy thermometer, drop a bit of the sugar mixture into a cup of ice water. If the mixture forms a soft ball, it's ready.

Pour the mixture slowly into the egg whites. Increase the mixer speed to high and beat until the mixture cools completely. It should be at room temperature. Add the butter and mix well. (The buttercream is now ready to use, or can be covered and

stored in the refrigerator for up to 2 weeks. Bring to room temperature before using.)

Mix the remaining cream of coconut with the $^1/_4$ cup water.

To assemble the cake, place 1 layer on a serving plate and top with half of the diluted cream of coconut. Spoon half of the pastry cream onto the layer, spreading evenly. Top with the second layer, topping it with the remaining cream of coconut and pastry cream. Place the third layer on top and frost the top and sides of the cake with the buttercream frosting. Cover the top and sides of the cake with the toasted coconut.

SERVES 6 TO 8

KULA STRAWBERRY SHORTCAKE

Here is my favorite way to showcase the beautiful strawberries from farmer Roy Hamamura in Kula, my favorite strawberry guy. Yum! — *T.G.*

WHITE BUTTER CAKE

3 cups cake flour

1¹/2 cups granulated sugar

1 tablespoon plus 1 teaspoon baking powder

³/4 teaspoon salt

6 egg yolks

1 cup milk

2¹/2 teaspoons vanilla extract

³/4 cup unsalted butter, at room temperature

2 pints fresh strawberries, hulled

1 cup simple syrup (page 44)

2 cups heavy cream

¹/4 cup confectioners' sugar

¹/2 teaspoon vanilla extract

¹/2 cup strawberry jam

1 cup pastry cream (page 184)

Preheat the oven to 350°. Butter and flour a 9-cup Bundt pan. To prepare the cake, in a bowl, sift together the flour, sugar, baking powder, and salt. In another bowl, mix together the egg yolks, ¹/2 cup of the milk, and the vanilla until blended. Add the butter and the remaining ¹/2 cup milk to the dry mixture and, using an electric mixer on medium-low speed, beat for about 3 minutes, until a smooth meal forms. Scrape down the sides of the bowl. Slowly add the yolk mixture to the flour mixture in 3 batches, making sure to scrape down the sides of the bowl after each addition.

Pour into the prepared Bundt pan and bake for 45 to 50 minutes, until the cake springs back to the touch. Invert the cake onto a rack immediately and allow to cool. Using a serrated knife, cut the cake horizontally into 2 layers.

In a blender, purée 4 to 6 strawberries until smooth. Add the simple syrup and process to mix. Lay each cake layer on a plate and, with a pastry brush, brush half of the purée on the bottom of the top layer and the remainder on the top of the bottom layer.

In a bowl, combine the cream, confectioners' sugar, and vanilla and whip until stiff peaks form.

To assemble the cake, spread the strawberry jam on the bottom layer. Top with the pastry cream.

Cut the remaining strawberries in half lengthwise and place all but 10 (reserve the largest and nicest) of the strawberry halves, cut-side down, on top of the pastry cream. Spoon ²/3 of the whipped cream into a pastry bag fitted with a small star tip and pipe the cream attractively on top of the strawberries. Cover with the top layer of cake. Fill the hole in the center with the remaining whipped cream and the reserved strawberries.

SERVES 6

❧ The beautiful strawberries I get, which are grown on the slopes of Mount Haleakalā, are red all the way to the top of the berry. It's a quality you should look for at your market, because it means the berries are sweet.

LEMON CREPES WITH RASPBERRY COMPOTE

I was looking for a light dessert in which to incorporate fresh raspberries grown in Kula. I recommend that the crepes be served with sorbet. Liliko'i, pineapple, and guava will all complement the lemon. — T.G.

LEMON CREPES

1 cup flour

2 tablespoons granulated sugar

1/4 teaspoon salt

2 eggs

1 1/2 cups milk

1/2 cup heavy cream

1 tablespoon chopped lemon zest

RASPBERRY COMPOTE

1 1/2 cups simple syrup (see note)

2 pints fresh raspberries

1/4 cup cornstarch

1 tablespoon water

2 tablespoons clarified butter (page 167), melted

1 1/2 cups pastry cream (page 184), flavored with a favorite liqueur, if desired

1/4 cup confectioners' sugar, for dusting

To prepare the crepe batter, in a bowl, combine the flour, granulated sugar, and salt. Add the eggs, one at a time, whisking well after each addition. Slowly whisk in the milk and then add the cream. Strain through a fine-mesh sieve into a clean bowl, cover, and refrigerate for about 2 hours. Stir in the lemon zest.

To prepare the compote, in a saucepan, heat the simple syrup and half of the raspberries over medium heat. Bring to a boil, remove from the heat, and strain through a fine-mesh sieve into a bowl. Return to the same saucepan, place over medium heat, and return to a boil.

In a small bowl, stir together the cornstarch and water. Pour into the raspberry mixture and stir until it comes to a rolling boil. Remove from the heat and let cool slightly. Mix in the remaining raspberries. Keep warm until serving.

To cook, brush an 8- or 10-inch crepe pan with some of the clarified butter. Ladle in 1/4 cup of the crepe batter and tilt the pan to coat the bottom evenly. Cook for about 2 minutes, until the edges start to brown. Carefully flip and cook the other side for 2 minutes, until set. Transfer to a plate. Repeat until all the crepe batter is used. You should have 12 crepes.

Spoon 2 tablespoons of the pastry cream onto each crepe and fold into a triangle. If you'd like, reheat the filled crepes in a 350° oven.

Transfer 2 crepes to each individual plate and ladle 6 tablespoons of the raspberry compote over each serving. Dust the crepes with confectioners' sugar and serve.

SERVES 6

To make 1 1/2 cups of SIMPLE SYRUP, combine 2/3 cup water and 1 1/2 cups sugar in a small saucepan. Stir to dissolve the sugar, then bring to a boil for 2 minutes, until thickened.

Oops. No room for the crab dip recipe in spring.
Better luck in summer.

Summer Recipes to Cool the Soul

Appetizers

Sashimi Napoleon, 51

Rock Shrimp Lumpia with Green Papaya Salad, 52

Macadamia Nut–Crusted Soft-Shell Crab with Spicy Pineapple Slaw, 53

Thai Ahi Tartare with Sprout Salad, 54

Chicken Satay with Peanut Dipping Sauce, 56

Gazpacho Terrine with Spicy Crab Salad, 57

Soups

Gazpacho, 58

Tortilla Soup, 59

Summer Tomato-Basil Soup, 60

Seafood Saimin, 61

Salads

Our Famous House Salad, 62

Chinese Chicken Salad, 63

Paella Salad, 65

Summer Chopped Salad, 66

ENTRÉES

Macadamia Nut–Crusted Ono with Mango-Lime Butter, 67

Grilled Ono with Mango-Corn Salsa, 68

Miso-Glazed Grilled Monchong with Sesame-Honey-Ginger Slaw, 70

Grilled Ahi with Asian Ratatouille, 71

Soft-Shell Tacos with Salmon, Avocado Salsa, and Spicy Cherry Tomato Salad, 72

Cabo Wabo–Marinated Grilled Chicken Breasts with Pineapple-Citrus Salsa, 74

Chicken with Artichokes, Sundried Tomatoes, and Pine Nuts, 75

Kālua Pork Enchiladas, Chile Verde Style, 77

DESSERTS

Exotic Fresh Fruit Tart, 78

White Chocolate–Raspberry Soufflé Cake, 79

Frozen Lemongrass Crème Brûlée in a Ginger Phyllo Tulip, 80

Mango-Pineapple Cobbler, 83

Macadamia Nut Lace Tulip Filled with Assorted Tropical Sorbets, 84

Maui-resident Karen Jennings is a well-known ceramic artist. She came in for dinner one night not long after we opened and said, "A big school of my fish would look great there," as she gestured to the blank wall around the kitchen. We couldn't afford to buy her brightly colored ceramic fish, but she decided to hang them in the store anyway. It's proven to be great exposure for her artwork, and she sells almost as many fish out of the restaurant as we sell of our fresh catch of the day! 🌺

SASHIMI NAPOLEON

HGS CLASSIC

After a trip to Gotham Bar & Grill in New York City, I came back feeling as if I had to put a vertical dish on the menu! Servers who work at Hali'imaile General Store must be trained at both carrying and then smashing-to-perfection this signature plate. It has appeared in Travel & Leisure *magazine because it's as stunning to look at as it is delicious. Although this is not as tall as the incredible creations of Gotham chef Alfred Portale, I think he'd approve.*

3/4 pound sashimi-grade tuna

1 bunch radish sprouts

8 shiso leaves

1/4 pound smoked salmon, thinly sliced

1/2 cup sliced pickled ginger, for garnish

1 tablespoon tobiko (flying fish roe), for garnish

TARTARE BASE

2 tablespoons good-quality mayonnaise

1 teaspoon Vietnamese garlic-chile sauce

2 tablespoons chopped green onion, white and
    green parts

2 teaspoons tobiko (flying fish roe)

1 tablespoon chopped fresh cilantro

CRISPY WONTONS

18 (3 inch-square) wonton skins

Peanut oil, for frying

DRESSING

2 tablespoons rice vinegar

2 tablespoons soy sauce

1/2 cup olive oil

2 tablespoons wasabi paste

2 teaspoons ground toasted sesame seeds (page 63)

Cut 1/4 pound of the tuna against the grain into 12 thin slices. Finely chop the other 1/2 pound for the tartare.

To prepare the tartare base, combine all the ingredients and mix well. Add the chopped fish and stir lightly to combine.

To prepare the crispy wontons, in a saucepan, pour in the oil to a depth of 1 inch and heat to 375°. Add the wonton skins and fry, turning once, for 8 to 10 seconds on each side, until light golden brown. Keep the wontons flat by using tongs to uncurl them. Using a wire skimmer, transfer to paper towels to drain. Allow to cool.

To prepare the dressing, in a bowl, combine all the ingredients and mix well.

To assemble, first roll the tuna slices up into rose-shaped bundles. Reserving 2 tablespoons of the radish sprouts, stack in the following order: wonton skin, one-sixth of the tartare mixture, shiso leaf, wonton skin, one-sixth of the smoked salmon, radish sprouts, wonton skin, 2 tuna rolls.

Sprinkle the top of each napoleon with the reserved radish sprouts. Drizzle 3 tablespoons of the dressing around each plate. Garnish with pickled ginger and tobiko.

To serve, cut through the entire stack with a knife, and smash the layers together with a fork to blend the flavors.

_____

SERVES 6

🍃 Shiso is unlike any other flavor. I describe it as an aromatic Japanese mint. You can find shiso leaves at a Japanese market, or try begging your local sushi bar to sell you a few!

ROCK SHRIMP LUMPIA
WITH GREEN PAPAYA SALAD

People tend to share appetizers at our restaurant, so we always need to have starters on the menu than can be split for two to four people. This is one of them. We actually planted papaya trees outside the restaurant. Over the years, they have provided us with many of the green papayas we shred for the salad that accompanies this dish. Lumpia wrappers are very thin flour-based square wrappers from the Philippines.

GREEN PAPAYA SALAD

1 red onion, sliced

2 green papayas, seeded, peeled, and shredded

2 carrots, peeled and shredded

2 teaspoons Vietnamese garlic-chile sauce

3 cloves garlic, minced

3 tablespoons sugar

2 tablespoons fish sauce

2 tablespoons rice vinegar

2 tablespoons freshly squeezed lime juice

1/4 cup chopped fresh cilantro

1/4 cup chopped fresh mint

1/4 cup chopped peanuts, for garnish

2 pounds peeled rock shrimp

1 tablespoon peanut oil, plus extra for brushing

2 1/2 teaspoons Asian sesame oil

1 (4-ounce) package Japanese rice noodles

1/2 cup peeled and shredded carrot

3/4 cup good-quality mayonnaise

1 teaspoon rice vinegar

2 tablespoons toasted sesame seeds (page 63)

2 teaspoons Vietnamese garlic-chile sauce

2 teaspoons salt

1/2 cup chopped fresh cilantro

12 (7-inch-square) lumpia wrappers

1 egg beaten with 1 tablespoon water, for egg wash

To prepare the salad, place the onion, papaya, and carrots in a bowl and mix well. In another bowl, combine the chile sauce, garlic, sugar, fish sauce, vinegar, and lime juice. Adjust the seasoning. Pour the chile sauce mixture over the papaya mixture and toss well. Add the cilantro and mint and toss well. Garnish with the peanuts.

Squeeze any excess moisture out of the shrimp. In a small pan, heat the 1 tablespoon peanut oil and 2 teaspoons of the sesame oil over medium-high heat. Add the shrimp and sauté for 3 to 4 minutes, until pink and starting to curl. Drain the shrimp in a colander and set aside. Bring a saucepan filled with water to a boil. Place the rice noodles in a bowl and pour the boiling water over them. Allow to soak for 5 minutes, until softened. Drain and set aside.

Preheat the oven to 450°.

Mix together the shrimp, rice noodles, carrot, mayonnaise, remaining 1/2 teaspoon sesame oil, vinegar, sesame seeds, chile sauce, and salt. Add the cilantro and mix well.

To prepare each lumpia, lay a wrapper on a clean work surface with the point facing you. Spread 2 tablespoons of the shrimp mixture evenly on the bottom one-third of each lumpia wrapper. Brush all 4 edges with the egg wash. Fold the bottom up over the filling and fold in the sides toward the middle. Starting at the bottom, roll up to form a tidy bundle. Repeat with the remaining filling and wrappers. Brush with peanut oil.

Place the lumpia on a baking sheet and bake for 10 to 12 minutes, until golden brown.

To serve, place 1/2 cup of the salad on each plate. Cut the lumpia in half diagonally. Stand 4 pieces of lumpia, point up, on each plate around the salad.

SERVES 6

MACADAMIA NUT–CRUSTED SOFT-SHELL CRAB WITH SPICY PINEAPPLE SLAW

Being a lover of soft-shell crab, I wanted to create a unique, island-flavored dish using this shellfish. When fried, the macadamia nut breading creates a really crunchy, juicy sensation. The pineapple slaw, although spicy, is a cooling complement.

SPICY PINEAPPLE SLAW

1/4 cup good-quality mayonnaise

2 tablespoons sour cream

1 teaspoon rice vinegar

1 tablespoon soy sauce

1 teaspoon sambal (Indonesian garlic-chile paste)

2 tablespoons Asian sesame oil

1 tablespoon peeled and minced fresh ginger

3 cups thinly sliced won bok (Chinese cabbage)

1/2 cup thinly sliced red cabbage

1/4 cup peeled and grated carrot

1/4 cup golden raisins

1/4 cup fresh pineapple chunks

2 tablespoons coriander seeds, ground

2 tablespoons mustard seeds, ground

2 teaspoons five-spice powder

1/2 cup macadamia nut pieces, toasted and finely ground (page 106)

1/2 cup panko (Japanese bread crumbs), crushed

1/2 teaspoon salt

1/2 teaspoon freshly ground black pepper

Peanut oil, for frying

4 eggs

1/4 cup milk

1 cup flour

4 soft-shell crabs

To prepare the slaw, in a bowl, combine the mayonnaise, sour cream, vinegar, soy sauce, chile paste, sesame oil, and ginger. Mix well. In another bowl, combine the won bok, red cabbage, carrot, raisins, and pineapple and stir to mix. Add to the mayonnaise mixture and toss to coat evenly.

To prepare the coating, in a bowl, mix together the coriander, mustard, five-spice powder, macadamia nuts, and panko. Season with salt and pepper.

In a heavy saucepan, pour in the oil to a depth of 2 inches and heat to 350°.

In a bowl, whisk together the eggs and milk. Pour the flour into a shallow bowl. To bread the crabs, dust them lightly with flour and shake off any excess. Dip the floured crab into the milk mixture and coat, then dip them into the nut mixture and coat evenly. Add the crabs to the hot oil and, working in batches, fry for 2 minutes on each side, until golden brown. Using tongs, transfer to paper towels to drain.

To serve, divide the slaw evenly among individual plates. Place a crab on top of each bed of slaw, and serve immediately.

SERVES 4

🖎 Most people don't have access to fresh soft-shell crabs, and their season is short in any case. Frozen soft-shell crabs are completely acceptable.

THAI AHI TARTARE WITH SPROUT SALAD

After a cooking journey to Bangkok, I had to marry the flavors I learned about in Thailand with the fresh raw fish of our islands. This is the result.

1/2 pound sashimi-grade ahi (yellowfin), cut into 11/2 by 2 by 6-inch blocks

1/4 cup radish sprouts

1/4 cup sunflower sprouts or radish sprouts

1/4 cup mung bean sprouts

1/4 cup peeled and shredded carrot

1 teaspoon freshly squeezed lemon juice

1/2 teaspoon Asian sesame oil

11/2 teaspoons freshly squeezed lime juice

1/2 teaspoon finely chopped lime zest

1 tablespoon fish sauce

1/4 teaspoon Sriracha (Thai garlic-chile paste)

1 tablespoon plus 11/2 teaspoons olive oil

1 teaspoon honey

Pinch of salt

Pinch of freshly ground black pepper

1 teaspoon sugar

1 tablespoon chopped dry-roasted peanuts

2 tablespoons chopped fresh cilantro

Cut the ahi into thin slices, slightly on the bias, and fan on individual plates, dividing equally. In a bowl, combine the sprouts and carrots and toss with the lemon juice and sesame oil. Arrange on the plates, slightly overlapping the fish slices.

In a small bowl, combine the lime juice, lime zest, fish sauce, chile paste, olive oil, honey, salt, pepper, and sugar and mix well. Drizzle this sauce over the fish. Sprinkle the fish with the peanuts and cilantro. Serve at once.

SERVES 4

🌀 I use sambal (Indonesian garlic-chile paste) or Sriracha (Thai garlic-chile paste) to give a good, hot, spicy taste to many of my dishes. A little bit goes a long way. Both pastes are readily available at Asian markets or the Asian food section of large supermarkets.

CHICKEN SATAY WITH PEANUT DIPPING SAUCE

We serve some version of satay at just about every party we cater. The sauce, which is one of my favorites, gives adults a great excuse to eat peanut butter!

PEANUT DIPPING SAUCE

1/3 cup chunky peanut butter

2/3 cup frozen coconut milk, thawed

1 clove garlic, minced

1 lemongrass stalk, white part only, minced

1/2 teaspoon fish sauce

1/2 teaspoon soy sauce

1 teaspoon sambal (Indonesian garlic-chile paste)

1 pound boneless, skinless chicken breast halves

Salt

Freshly ground black pepper

3 cloves garlic

1 tablespoon peeled and minced fresh ginger

2 teaspoons grated lime zest

1 teaspoon coriander seeds, toasted and ground (page 63)

1 cup frozen coconut milk, thawed

To prepare the peanut sauce, in a saucepan, combine all the ingredients over low heat. Simmer, stirring frequently, for 10 minutes, until thick. Transfer to a bowl and allow to cool.

Soak 16 bamboo skewers in water for at least 20 minutes. Prepare a fire in a charcoal grill, or preheat a gas grill.

Cut the chicken lengthwise into 4-inch strips. Remove the skewers from the water and thread the chicken on them. Season the chicken with salt and pepper and lay in a shallow dish.

To prepare the marinade, in a blender, combine the garlic, ginger, lime zest, and coriander seeds. Add the coconut milk and blend until smooth. Pour the marinade over the chicken skewers and marinate for 15 to 20 minutes.

Place the skewers on the grill rack and grill, turning once, for about 5 minutes, until cooked through. Serve with the peanut sauce.

SERVES 4

✿ Soaking bamboo skewers in water before using them keeps them from burning on the grill.

GAZPACHO TERRINE WITH SPICY CRAB SALAD

Every baby boomer should be nostalgic about the taste of molded salads. I literally begged for the recipe of one I ate at a friend's home. She was kind enough to share it, and I've adapted it for our use. Thanks, Bubba!

GAZPACHO TERRINE

1/3 cup chopped yellow bell pepper

6 large, ripe tomatoes, peeled, seeded, and chopped

1 cucumber, peeled, seeded, and diced

1 1/2 cups tomato juice

1 teaspoon salt

1/2 teaspoon freshly ground black pepper

4 teaspoons unflavored gelatin dissolved in 1/4 cup hot water

SPICY CRAB SALAD

1 pound cooked crabmeat

1/2 cup chopped celery

1 tablespoon chopped pimiento

1 tablespoon chopped fresh dill

1/2 cup good-quality mayonnaise

1/2 cup peeled and shredded carrot

1 teaspoon Tabasco sauce

1/4 cup olive oil

1 tablespoon plus 1 1/2 teaspoons rice vinegar

1 teaspoon salt

1/4 teaspoon freshly ground black pepper

1 tablespoon chopped green onion, green part only

4 cups shredded red cabbage

16 sprigs cilantro, for garnish

To prepare the gazpacho terrine, bring a large saucepan filled with salted water to a boil over high heat. Using a slotted spoon or wire skimmer, drop in the bell pepper and blanch for 1 to 2 minutes, until al dente. Drain in a colander and allow to cool.

In a bowl, combine the bell pepper, tomatoes, cucumber, tomato juice, salt, and pepper. In a small saucepan, soften the gelatin over low heat. Remove from the heat, allow to cool, and add to the tomato mixture. Spray an 8 1/2 by 4 1/2-inch loaf pan with vegetable-oil cooking spray, then line with plastic wrap, leaving some extra wrap overlapping the edges. Add the tomato mixture and tap the pan several times on the counter to release any bubbles. Cover with the overlapping plastic wrap and refrigerate overnight, until firm.

To prepare the salad, in a large bowl, combine the crab, celery, pimiento, dill, mayonnaise, and carrot and mix well. In small bowl, combine the Tabasco, oil, vinegar, salt, pepper, and green onion and mix well. Add to the crab mixture and toss well.

To unmold the terrine, invert onto a plate and lift off the pan. Peel off the plastic wrap. Slice and place on a bed of red cabbage. Top with one eighth of the crab salad. Garnish each serving with 2 cilantro sprigs.

SERVES 8

GAZPACHO

I bet I've eaten a thousand bowls of gazpacho in varying forms. No matter where you grew up or live now and no matter what your ethnicity, it's a refreshing summer dish.

1 pound ripe tomatoes, peeled, seeded, and
   finely chopped

1/2 cup chopped onion

1/2 cup chopped red bell pepper

1/2 cup chopped yellow bell pepper

3/4 cup peeled, seeded, and chopped cucumber

4 cups tomato juice

1/4 cup freshly squeezed lemon juice

1 tablespoon freshly squeezed lime juice

2 tablespoons olive oil

1 tablespoon salt

1/4 teaspoon freshly ground black pepper

2 tablespoons chopped fresh cilantro, for garnish

2 tablespoons chopped green onion, white and
   green parts, for garnish

2 tablespoons crème frâiche (page 60), for garnish

In a large bowl, combine the tomatoes, onion, bell peppers, and cucumber and mix well.

In a blender, combine the tomato juice, lemon juice, lime juice, and olive oil and blend on low speed for 1 minute, until well blended. Pour over the tomato mixture and mix well. Season with salt and pepper. Cover and refrigerate until well chilled. Taste and adjust the seasoning before serving. Ladle into chilled bowls and garnish with the cilantro, green onion, and crème frâiche.

SERVES 6

TORTILLA SOUP

*I know there are many versions of tortilla soup on menus in restaurants all over the country. Of course,
I think ours is one of the best, and, judging by the number of requests we get for it, our customers agree.*

GOAT CHEESE CREAM

1/4 cup fresh goat cheese, at room temperature

About 2 tablespoons heavy cream

4 tablespoons olive oil

*1/2 pound chicken breast meat, cut into
narrow strips*

Salt

Freshly ground black pepper

1 onion, chopped

6 corn tortillas, cut into strips

1 tablespoon minced garlic

6 cups chicken stock (see page 10)

2 cups peeled, seeded, and coarsely chopped tomato

2 cups tomato purée

1 tablespoon ground cumin

1 tablespoon chile powder

1 tablespoon minced chipotle chile in adobo

Corn oil, for frying

2 tablespoons coarsely chopped fresh cilantro

Pepitas (toasted pumpkin seeds), for garnish

To prepare the goat cheese cream, in a bowl, mix the ingredients together, adding cream to desired consistency.

To prepare the soup, in a skillet, heat 2 tablespoons of the oil over medium-high heat. Add the chicken strips and sauté for 4 minutes, until tender. Season with salt and pepper and set aside.

In a saucepan, heat the remaining 2 tablespoons oil. Add the onion and sauté for 3 minutes, until translucent. Add one-half of the tortilla strips and continue to cook for about 4 minutes, until they fall apart, then add the garlic.

Add the chicken stock, tomato, and tomato purée and stir well. Then add the cumin, chile powder, and chipotle chile and bring to a boil. Decrease the heat to low and simmer, covered, for 25 minutes.

Meanwhile, in a sauté pan, pour in the corn oil to a depth of 1/2 inch and heat over high heat to 350°. Add the remaining one-half tortilla strips and fry for 30 to 45 seconds, until golden brown and crispy. Using a slotted spoon, transfer to paper towels to drain.

Remove the soup from the heat and, working in batches, purée in a blender. Return to the saucepan, add the cilantro, and stir well. Ladle into warmed bowls and garnish with the fried tortilla strips, chicken strips, and *pepitas*. Drizzle with the goat cheese cream.

SERVES 6

Our Famous House Salad

HGS Classic

I've been making this salad for thirty years, and even though one reviewer took me to task for using canned mandarin oranges, it's the combination of all the different ingredients that makes it so good. On the other end of the spectrum, one of our customers raced home to re-create it after she tasted it for the first time in the week or so after we opened.

House Dressing

3/4 cup olive oil

3/4 cup canola oil

1/3 cup balsamic vinegar

1/3 cup rice vinegar

2 tablespoons Dijon mustard

1 tablespoon dried tarragon

2 tablespoons sugar

1 tablespoon freshly squeezed lemon juice

1/4 teaspoon salt

1/4 pound mixed baby salad greens

24 mandarin orange sections

1/2 cup walnut pieces, toasted (page 106)

1/2 small Maui onion, thinly sliced

1/2 cup crumbled blue cheese

To prepare the dressing, combine the oils in a pitcher and set aside. Combine the remaining dressing ingredients in a bowl. Using an electric mixer on low speed, drizzle in the oils as the other ingredients are being mixed.

In a large bowl, toss the salad greens with 1/4 cup of the dressing. Divide among 4 plates. Divide the oranges, walnuts, onion, and blue cheese evenly on top of the salads. Serve at once.

SERVES 4

✍ This dressing is so good that it's worth making the extra to have in the fridge as an all-purpose salad dressing. It goes well with just about any kind of salad and will keep for up to 3 weeks in the refrigerator.

CHINESE CHICKEN SALAD

HGS CLASSIC

This dish is so popular it frequently shows up on the menus of other restaurants. Now that the recipe is published, I guess it will show up on even more restaurant menus! Imitation is the sincerest form of flattery, right?

DRESSING

2 teaspoons olive oil

1 tablespoon chopped shallot

2 tablespoons dry white wine

1/4 cup mango chutney

1 (16-ounce) bottle Hawaiian Tropics Oriental Dressing or any Asian sesame ginger dressing

2 tablespoons sesame seeds, toasted (see note)

WONTON CHIPS

Peanut oil, for deep-frying

10 (3-inch-square) wonton skins, cut into 1/4-inch-wide strips

1 pound boneless, skinless chicken breast halves

1 red bell pepper, seeded and julienned

1/3 cup sliced water chestnuts

5 cups mixed salad greens

1/2 cup shredded coconut, toasted

1/2 cup dry-roasted peanuts

1/2 cup raisins

Prepare a fire in a charcoal grill, or preheat a gas grill.

To prepare the dressing, in a skillet, heat the olive oil over medium heat. Add the shallots and sauté for 3 minutes, until translucent. Add the wine, chutney, and bottled dressing and heat through. Add the sesame seeds. Allow to cool.

To prepare the wonton chips, in a saucepan, pour in the oil to a depth of 2 inches and heat to 350°. Add the wonton strips to the oil, a few at a time. They will fry very fast, taking only about 15 seconds to get crispy. Using a slotted spoon, transfer to paper towels to drain.

Place the chicken on the grill rack and grill, turning as needed, for 10 to 20 minutes, until done. Cut into strips and allow to cool.

In a bowl, combine the chicken strips, bell pepper, and water chestnuts. Add 1/2 cup of the dressing to coat the mixture.

In another bowl, toss the salad greens lightly with 1/2 cup of the dressing. (The remaining dressing can be stored for up to 30 days in an airtight container in the refrigerator.)

Divide the greens among 6 plates, and top each with one-sixth of the chicken mixture. Sprinkle each salad with the coconut, peanuts, raisins, and wonton chips. Serve immediately.

SERVES 6

🍂 Always lightly TOAST SESAME SEEDS to bring out their flavor: Heat a dry sauté pan over high heat. Add sesame seeds and toast, swirling the pan often, for about 2 minutes, until light golden in color. Remove from the pan immediately to prevent burning and allow to cool before using. This method can also be used to TOAST SPICE SEEDS such as coriander.

Paella Salad

I created this dish for a Hawai'i Nature Center benefit for five hundred people. It was a cold buffet, and I came up with a great combination of seafood, chicken, and rice that has become a popular part of our catering repertoire. People who attended that event—several years ago now—are still talking about this dish.

RICE

2 tablespoons olive oil

1 cup jasmine rice

2¹/2 cups chicken stock (see page 10)

Pinch of saffron threads

³/4 teaspoon salt

¹/2 cup extra virgin olive oil

¹/4 cup julienned red bell pepper

¹/4 cup julienned yellow bell pepper

¹/2 pound shrimp, peeled and deveined

¹/4 pound sea scallops

¹/4 pound boneless, skinless chicken breast, cut into ¹/4-inch strips

¹/4 cup cooked and quartered artichoke hearts (page 183)

¹/4 cup sliced water chestnuts

¹/2 cup shelled green peas

2 tablespoons chopped fresh chives

2 tablespoons chopped fresh cilantro

1 teaspoon salt

¹/2 teaspoon freshly ground black pepper

¹/4 cup freshly squeezed lemon juice

Zest from 2 lemons, cut in strips

Sprigs of cilantro, for garnish

To prepare the rice, in a heavy saucepan, heat the oil over medium heat. Add the rice and stir constantly for about 6 minutes, until the kernels are opaque. Do not allow the rice to brown. Add the stock, saffron, and salt, stir well, and bring to a simmer. Cover, decrease the heat to low, and cook for 10 to 12 minutes, until the rice is tender and all the liquid has been absorbed. Transfer the rice to a large bowl and allow to cool.

To prepare the remaining ingredients, in a sauté pan, heat 2 tablespoons of the extra virgin olive oil over high heat. When hot, add the bell peppers and sauté for 3 minutes, until they take on a light brown color. Transfer to a plate to cool.

In the same pan, add 1 tablespoon of the olive oil and sauté the shrimp over high heat for 3 minutes, until they turn pink and start to curl. Transfer to a plate. Add another 1 tablespoon olive oil, add the scallops, and sauté for 3 minutes, until slightly firm to the touch. Transfer to the plate.

In another sauté pan, heat 1 tablespoon of the oil over medium-high heat. Add the chicken and sauté for 4 to 5 minutes, until it browns and cooks through.

In a bowl, combine the peppers, shrimp, scallops, artichoke hearts, water chestnuts, peas, chives, and cilantro. Season with salt and pepper. Add the remaining 3 tablespoons extra virgin olive oil and the lemon juice and zest. Let marinate for 20 minutes at room temperature.

Add the seafood-vegetable mixture and the chicken to the rice and toss to combine well, then serve, garnished with cilantro sprigs.

SERVES 4

🍃 Please don't fret about using frozen green peas. It's fine. I promise.

SUMMER CHOPPED SALAD

A chopped vegetable salad is a must on every summer menu. With all the incredible produce that's grown here now, the product in its purest form at the peak of its growing time needs nothing more than a little great extra virgin olive oil, a dash of fresh lemon juice, and some shaved Parmesan. The freshest of fresh flavors.

1/8 pound asparagus

1/8 pound green beans

1/4 cup corn kernels (from about 1/2 ear)

1/4 cup sliced red onion

1/4 pound zucchini, halved lengthwise

1/4 pound yellow squash, halved lengthwise

1/4 cup peeled, seeded, and chopped tomato

1/2 avocado, diced

1/4 cup extra virgin olive oil

1/2 cup freshly shaved Parmesan cheese

Salt

Freshly ground black pepper

1/4 pound baby arugula

CITRUS VINAIGRETTE

10 cloves roasted garlic (page 9)

1 tablespoon peeled and minced fresh ginger

2 tablespoons freshly squeezed lemon juice

1/2 cup olive oil

1 teaspoon salt

1/2 teaspoon white pepper

Prepare a fire in a charcoal grill, or preheat a gas grill.

Bring a large saucepan filled with salted water to a boil over high heat. Using a slotted spoon or wire skimmer, drop in the asparagus, green beans, and corn and blanch for 1 to 2 minutes, until al dente. Drain the vegetables in a colander and allow to cool.

Meanwhile, place the onion slices, zucchini, and yellow squash on the grill rack and grill, turning once, for 3 to 4 minutes total, until soft but not overcooked.

Cut all the cooked vegetables into 1/4-inch cubes. To prepare the salad, in a bowl, toss together the asparagus, beans, corn, onion, zucchini, yellow squash, tomato, and avocado. Drizzle in the olive oil, add the Parmesan, and toss to coat lightly. Season with salt and pepper.

To prepare the vinaigrette, in a bowl, whisk together all the ingredients.

Divide the arugula among 4 plates. Place an equal portion of the vegetable mixture on each bed of arugula. Drizzle the citrus vinaigrette on the salad.

SERVES 4

❧ The best Parmesan cheese you can buy is fresh Italian Parmigiano-Reggiano. Using a vegetable peeler is the easiest way to shave slices.

Macadamia Nut–Crusted Ono with Mango-Lime Butter

Twelve years later, our macadamia nut–crusted fish has won itself a permanent place on the menu. The type of fish changes with the season, but if this is the preparation you crave, you will never be disappointed.

MANGO-LIME BUTTER

1/2 cup chopped fresh mango
1/2 cup dry white wine
2 tablespoons sugar
1 teaspoon peeled and minced fresh ginger
Juice of 2 limes
1/4 cup heavy cream
1/2 cup cold unsalted butter, cut into small pieces
Salt
Freshly ground black pepper

1/2 cup macadamia nuts, whole or pieces
2 cups panko (Japanese bread crumbs)
1/2 cup fresh basil
1/2 cup good-quality mayonnaise
2 teaspoons Sriracha (Thai garlic-chile paste)
6 (6-ounce) ono fillets
Salt
Freshly ground black pepper
Canola oil, for sautéing

To prepare the mango-lime butter, in a saucepan, combine the mango, wine, sugar, ginger, and lime juice and simmer over medium heat for 5 minutes, until thick and syrupy. Add the cream, mix well, and remove from the heat. Pour into a blender and blend until smooth. Return to the saucepan and simmer over low heat for 8 minutes, until the mixture thickens slightly. Add the butter, a piece at a time, and stir until incorporated before adding the next piece. Be careful not to boil the sauce, or it will separate. Season with salt and pepper and keep warm.

Preheat the oven to 450°.

To prepare the coating, place the nuts, panko, and basil in a food processor and process until fine. Spread on a plate. In a bowl, combine the mayonnaise and chile paste and mix well. Lightly season the fish with salt and pepper. Evenly spread a light coat of the chile mayonnaise on one side of each fish fillet. Coat the same side evenly with the coating.

In an ovenproof sauté pan or skillet, pour in just enough oil to coat the bottom and heat over medium heat. (Be careful not to heat the pan too hot or the macadamia nuts will burn.) Add the fish, crust side down, and sauté for 3 minutes, until golden brown. Turn the fish and place in the oven for 5 minutes, until cooked through and firm to the touch.

Place the fillets on warmed individual plates. Serve with the mango-lime butter.

SERVES 6

🍃 You can substitute any firm white fish for the ono, which is also known as wahoo. *Ono* means "delicious" in Hawaiian. If you have a fresh mango, let it get very ripe. It will be sweet and juicy and make this sauce even more delicious.

GRILLED ONO
WITH MANGO-CORN SALSA

Sometimes it's best to keep things simple. This dish is a perfect example of letting the wonderful flavors of each component shine. A piece of grilled fresh fish paired with the ripest mango needs little more than the sun setting in the ocean to complete a perfect summer meal.

MANGO-CORN SALSA

1 tablespoon olive oil

1/2 cup fresh corn kernels (from about 1 ear)

2 cups fresh mango, cut into 1/2-inch cubes

1/2 cup diced red onion

1/2 cup seeded and chopped tomato

2 tablespoons grated lime zest

2 tablespoons freshly squeezed lime juice

2 tablespoons chopped fresh cilantro

1/2 teaspoon salt

1/2 teaspoon freshly ground black pepper

12 (6-ounce) ono fillets

Salt

Freshly ground black pepper

2 tablespoons olive oil

Lime slices, for garnish

Prepare a fire in a charcoal grill, or preheat a gas grill.

To prepare the salsa, in a sauté pan, heat the olive oil over high heat. Add the corn and sauté for 30 seconds, until just tender. Allow to cool. In a bowl, mix together the remaining ingredients, add the corn, mix well, and set aside. This salsa is best when made several hours before serving, to allow the flavors to marry together.

Season the fish fillets with salt and pepper and rub with oil. Place on the grill rack and grill, turning once, for 2 minutes on each side, until just opaque at the center.

Place 2 fillets on each individual plate, top with 1/2 cup of the salsa, garnish with the lime slices, and serve immediately.

_____

SERVES 6

🌿 If you have access to freshly picked corn, you do not have to cook it for the salsa. The corn grown in Kula that we use in the restaurant is so sweet that we can use it raw right off the cob!

MISO-GLAZED GRILLED MONCHONG WITH SESAME-HONEY-GINGER SLAW

This is another of those dishes indicative of Hawai'i Regional Cuisine through its combination of excellent local fish, Asian ingredients, contemporary preparation, and all variety of flavors and textures. You can substitute sea bass or marlin for the monchong, which is also known as pomfret.

MISO GLAZE

1/4 cup sugar

1/4 cup white miso

1/4 cup soy sauce

1/4 cup water

SESAME-HONEY-GINGER DRESSING

1 tablespoon peeled and chopped fresh ginger

2 tablespoons honey

2 teaspoons chopped fresh basil

2 teaspoons Dijon mustard

2 tablespoons rice vinegar

1 teaspoon Asian sesame oil

1/3 cup canola oil

Salt

Freshly ground black pepper

1 tablespoon sesame seeds, toasted (page 63)

6 (6-ounce) monchong steaks

Freshly ground black pepper

2 tablespoons olive oil

3/4 cup peeled and shredded carrot

6 cups shredded won bok (Chinese cabbage)

1/2 cup julienned green onion, green part only

1 cup sunflower sprouts or radish sprouts

2 tablespoons finely chopped dry-roasted peanuts, for garnish

To prepare the miso glaze, in a bowl, whisk together all the ingredients until the sugar is incorporated. Set aside.

Prepare a fire in a charcoal grill, or preheat a gas grill.

To prepare the dressing, in a blender, combine the ginger, honey, basil, mustard, and vinegar and blend until smooth. With the motor running, slowly add the oils, blending well until emulsified. Season with salt and pepper and add the sesame seeds. Taste and add more honey if you want a sweeter dressing.

Reserving 6 teaspoons of the miso glaze, rub the fish steaks with the pepper and olive oil and coat with the glaze. Allow to sit at room temperature for 10 minutes before grilling.

In a bowl, combine the carrot, cabbage, green onion, and sprouts. Toss with the dressing just before serving to ensure that the slaw will be crisp.

Place the fish on the grill rack and grill, turning once, for 2 minutes on each side for medium rare.

To serve, place 1/2 cup of the slaw on each plate and lay a fish fillet over the slaw. Drizzle 1 teaspoon of the reserved miso glaze over each serving, and garnish with the peanuts.

SERVES 6

✿ Miso is a fermented soybean paste with a unique flavor. When using miso, season meat or fish lightly because it is inherently salty.

The sweet dressing made here is great on spinach or coleslaw, especially when served with savory meats like roast pork.

GRILLED AHI
WITH ASIAN RATATOUILLE

For years, there was always a bowl of ratatouille in my fridge. You could take a big spoonful out and serve it with almost anything, cold or hot. The Asian twist was inevitable.

1/4 cup olive oil, plus 2 tablespoons for
    brushing fish

2 Maui onions, thinly sliced

3 cloves garlic, minced

2 tablespoons finely chopped lemongrass,
    white part only

2 tablespoons peeled and minced fresh ginger

1 medium globe eggplant, cut into 1 inch cubes

1 red bell pepper, seeded and julienned

1 yellow bell pepper, seeded and julienned

2 zucchini, sliced 1/4 inch thick

2 yellow crookneck squashes, cut into
    1/4-inch pieces

1 tablespoon chopped fresh basil

1 tablespoon chopped fresh cilantro

3 ripe tomatoes, seeded and chopped

1/2 pound shiitake mushrooms, sliced

2 teaspoons salt

1 teaspoon freshly ground black pepper

1 tablespoon Asian sesame oil

3 tablespoons sesame seeds, toasted (page 63)

6 (6-ounce) ahi (yellowfin) steaks

CILANTRO-LIME SOUR CREAM

1/3 cup sour cream

1 tablespoon chopped fresh cilantro

1 tablespoon freshly squeezed lime juice

To prepare the ratatouille, in a large saucepan, heat the 1/4 cup oil over medium-high heat. Add the onions and sauté for 3 minutes, until translucent. Add the garlic, lemongrass, ginger, and eggplant and cook for 10 minutes, until the eggplant softens. Add the bell peppers, zucchini, and crookneck squashes, cover, and cook for 15 minutes, until fork tender, but not mushy. Meanwhile, prepare a fire in a charcoal grill, or preheat a gas grill.

Add the basil, cilantro, tomatoes, and mushrooms to the rest of the vegetables and cook, uncovered, for 10 minutes longer, until the mushrooms are tender. Season with salt and pepper. Add the sesame oil and sesame seeds.

Brush the ahi with the 2 tablespoons oil, place on the grill rack and grill, turning once, for 3 minutes on each side for medium rare.

To prepare the cilantro-lime cream, in a small bowl, combine all the ingredients and mix well. Spoon some ratatouille onto each plate and top with an ahi steak. Garnish with the cilantro-lime sour cream.

SERVES 6

Soft-Shell Tacos with Salmon, Avocado Salsa, and Spicy Cherry Tomato Salad

When I come into the restaurant and sit down at the bar after a long day of work and nothing on the menu appeals to me (yes, it does happen!), Chef Tom puts a perfectly cooked piece of salmon, some cheese, and a spicy tomato salad on a warm homemade tortilla. At that moment, nothing could be better.

Avocado Salsa

2 large or 3 small ripe avocados (not too soft), halved, pitted, peeled, and cut into $^1/4$-inch chunks

1 Maui onion or red onion, chopped

1 large ripe tomato, seeded and chopped

1 small jalapeño chile, seeded and finely chopped

$^1/4$ cup chopped fresh cilantro

1 tablespoon canola oil

Juice of 1 lemon

Salt

Freshly ground black pepper

Spicy Cherry Tomato Salad

1 pint cherry tomatoes, halved

1 red onion, julienned or chopped

1 small bunch cilantro, coarsely chopped

$^1/2$ chipotle chile in adobo, finely chopped

1 tablespoon olive oil

Juice of 1 lime

Salt

Freshly ground black pepper

Flour Tortillas

3 cups flour

$1^1/2$ teaspoons salt

$1^1/2$ teaspoons baking powder

4 tablespoons unsalted butter, at room temperature

$^3/4$ cup warm tap water

$^1/2$ cup sour cream

2 tablespoons chopped fresh cilantro

6 (5-ounce) salmon fillets

$^1/4$ cup canola oil

Salt

Freshly ground black pepper

1 cup shredded Monterey Jack cheese

1 cup shredded iceberg lettuce

To prepare the salsa, in a nonreactive bowl, combine all the ingredients, including salt and pepper to taste, and mix well. Set aside.

To prepare the salad, in a nonreactive bowl, combine all the ingredients including salt and pepper to taste, and mix well. Set aside.

Prepare a fire in a charcoal grill, or preheat a gas grill.

To prepare the tortillas, in a bowl, sift together the flour, salt, and baking powder. Cut the butter into small pieces and add to the flour mixture. Mix in the butter with a fork until a coarse meal is achieved. (You could also use cold butter and mix it in a food processor until the mixture is in pea-sized clumps.) Slowly add the warm water, stirring and tossing with a fork, to form a dough. (Or add the water through the feed tube of the processor.)

Separate the dough into 12 equal parts and roll each into a ball. Allow the dough balls to rest at room temperature for 5 to 7 minutes. On a floured surface, press down a ball and then roll out into a 6-inch round. Repeat with the remaining balls. (You can also use a tortilla press.) In a nonstick pan, cook each tortilla over medium heat for 1 to $1^1/2$ minutes on each side, until brown spots appear. Cover with a towel to keep them warm. (You can also allow the tortillas to cool and reheat them later in the nonstick pan or a microwave.)

In a small bowl, combine the sour cream and cilantro and mix well. Cover and place in the refrigerator until serving.

Rub the salmon fillets with the canola oil and season with salt and pepper. Place on the grill rack and grill, turning once, for about 3 minutes on each side, until opaque at the center for medium rare.

Place the salmon on a serving platter and serve family style with the salsa, cherry tomato salad, cilantro sour cream, cheese, lettuce, and warm tortillas. Everyone makes his or her own taco.

SERVES 6

🍃 Always wear rubber gloves when working with jalapeños or other fiery chiles. And don't ever touch your eyes.

Cabo Wabo—Marinated Grilled Chicken Breasts with Pineapple-Citrus Salsa

This was one of the first chicken dishes we put on the menu. It harkened back to my Tex-Mex days of marinating meat in tequila and lime. When my friends Shep Gordon and Sammy Haggar (yes, the one from Van Halen) began producing their Cabo-Wabo brand tequila, the name of the dish and the tequila we use for it quickly changed. And there's nothing like a Texas Ruby Red—grapefruit, that is.

$^1/_2$ cup freshly squeezed lime juice

$^1/_4$ cup tequila

4 cloves garlic

1 bunch cilantro

1 tablespoon peeled and finely chopped fresh ginger

1 jalapeño chile, seeded

2 tablespoons white vinegar

1 tablespoon sugar

1 tablespoon salt

$1^1/_2$ cups olive oil

6 boneless, skinless chicken breast halves

Pineapple-Citrus Salsa

1 Texas Ruby Red grapefruit

1 orange

1 cup diced pineapple

1 small red onion, thinly sliced

2 tablespoons chopped fresh cilantro

1 jalapeño chile, seeded and finely chopped

2 teaspoons raspberry vinegar

2 teaspoons sugar

To prepare the marinade, in a food processor, combine the lime juice, tequila, garlic, cilantro, ginger, jalapeño, vinegar, sugar, and salt. Pulse 10 times. With the motor running, add the olive oil through the feed tube and process until emulsified. Reserve $^3/_4$ cup of the marinade to serve with the chicken.

Place the chicken breasts in a nonreactive bowl and pour the remaining marinade over them. Cover and marinate overnight in the refrigerator.

Prepare a fire in a charcoal grill, or preheat a gas grill.

To prepare the salsa, cut a thick slice off the top and bottom of the grapefruit and place the fruit upright. Thickly slice off the peel in strips, removing the white pith and membrane and revealing the fruit sections. Holding the peeled fruit in one hand over a bowl to capture the juices, cut on each side of the membrane to free each section, letting the sections drop into the bowl. Repeat with the orange. Add all the remaining salsa ingredients and stir to mix.

Remove the chicken from the marinade and place on the grill rack. Grill, turning once, for 7 minutes on each side, until done.

To serve, divide the citrus salsa evenly among individual plates. Place a chicken breast on top of the salsa and spoon 2 to 3 tablespoons of the reserved marinade over each serving.

Serves 6

🌿 Any "top shelf" tequila will do for this recipe. And be sure to remove all the pith from the citrus, so the salsa isn't bitter.

CHICKEN WITH ARTICHOKES, SUNDRIED TOMATOES, AND PINE NUTS

At one time this was our friend Gini Baldwin's favorite dish. It went on the menu as "Gini's Chicken." Whenever we took it off the menu and she called and asked us to put it back on, we did. This is great served with pasta, basmati rice, or wild rice. It is a very good, quick, and impressive "dinner party" dish.

3 tablespoons unsalted butter

1 clove garlic, chopped

1/4 cup julienned dry-pack sundried tomatoes

1 cup chicken stock (see page 10)

1 cup heavy cream

6 boneless, skinless chicken breasts halves

1 teaspoon salt

Freshly ground black pepper

1/2 cup cooked and quartered artichoke hearts (page 183)

2 tablespoons chopped green onion, white and green parts

1 teaspoon tomato paste

2 tablespoons finely shredded fresh basil, plus extra for garnish

1/4 cup pine nuts, toasted (page 106), for garnish

To prepare the sauce, in a saucepan, melt 2 tablespoons of the butter over medium-high heat. Add the garlic and sauté for 1 minute, until softened. Add the tomatoes and 3/4 cup of the stock. Decrease the heat to low and simmer for about 5 minutes, until the tomatoes are tender. Add the cream, increase the heat to medium-high, and bring to a boil, then decrease the heat to low and simmer for about 8 minutes, until the sauce thickens.

To prepare the chicken, in a skillet, melt the remaining 1 tablespoon butter over medium-high heat. Season the chicken breasts with salt and pepper, add to the pan, and sauté, turning as necessary, for 10 to 12 minutes, until done. Transfer to a plate and keep warm.

Add the artichoke hearts to the same pan over high heat and sauté for 3 minutes, until lightly browned. Add the green onion, mix well, and transfer to the plate holding the chicken. Add the remaining 1/4 cup stock to the pan and deglaze over high heat, stirring to dislodge any browned bits on the pan bottom.

Add the contents of the skillet to the sauce. Then add the tomato paste and 2 tablespoons of basil and reduce over low heat for 4 minutes, until thickened. Adjust the seasoning.

Arrange the chicken breasts and artichoke hearts on warmed individual plates and spoon the sauce over them. Garnish with the pine nuts and the additional basil.

SERVES 6

❦ The best choice is fresh artichoke hearts, next best is frozen, and if you've no choice, canned will do. Make sure they're not marinated.

Kālua Pork Enchiladas,
Chile Verde Style

My Tex-Mex youth rears its enchilada head! If Pancho Villa knew about kālua pork, I guarantee you that Mexicans would use it in all their pork dishes. Chef Tom's mole sauce is so good that it can be eaten with a spoon! Serve with avocado salsa and spicy cherry tomato salad (page 72).

1 (2¹/₂-pound) pork butt

3 cloves garlic, chopped

1¹/₂ teaspoons ground cumin

1¹/₂ teaspoons dried oregano

Salt

Freshly ground black pepper

1¹/₂ teaspoons liquid smoke

¹/₂ cup chopped onion

1 cup drained canned tomatillos

1 cup chicken stock (see page 10)

MOLE SAUCE

1¹/₂ teaspoons canola oil

¹/₂ onion, chopped

2 cloves garlic

1 large tomato, chopped

2 tablespoons pepitas (toasted
   pumpkin seeds)

1 teaspoon sugar

2 ancho chiles, toasted, softened in warm water

1 teaspoon dried oregano

¹/₂ teaspoon ground cinnamon

1¹/₂ cups chicken stock (see page 10)

2¹/₂ teaspoons cider vinegar

1¹/₂ ounces Mexican chocolate, grated

¹/₂ teaspoon salt

¹/₂ teaspoon freshly ground black pepper

8 corn tortillas

1 cup chicken stock, heated

1 cup shredded manchego cheese

To prepare the pork, preheat the oven to 350°. Place the pork butt in a roasting pan and season with the garlic, cumin, oregano, salt, pepper, and liquid smoke. Add the onion, tomatillos, and stock to the pan. Cover with aluminum foil and cook in the oven for 1¹/₂ hours. Uncover and cook for 30 minutes more, until fork tender. Remove the pan from the oven, transfer the pork to a plate, and allow to cool. Shred the pork and set aside.

While the pork is cooling, pour the contents of the roasting pan into a food processor and process to create a coarse purée. Season with salt and pepper. Reserving 1 cup of the purée, add the remainder to the shredded meat to moisten it.

To prepare the mole sauce, in a saucepan, heat the oil over medium-high heat. Add the onion, garlic, and tomato and sauté for 2 minutes, until softened. Add the *pepitas,* sugar, chiles, oregano, cinnamon, stock, vinegar, and chocolate. Simmer, uncovered, for 20 minutes, until thickened. Purée with a hand blender and season with salt and pepper.

To finish the dish, preheat the oven to 350°. Coat the bottom of a baking dish with the reserved pork sauce. Dip a tortilla in the hot chicken stock and place on a plate. Place about one-eighth of the pork near the edge and roll up into a cylinder. Place seam side down in the baking dish. Repeat until all the tortillas and pork are used.

Cover the enchiladas with the mole sauce. Sprinkle with the manchego cheese. Bake for 20 to 25 minutes, until bubbling hot. To serve, place 2 enchiladas on each plate and spoon the mole sauce from the bottom of the baking dish over each serving.

SERVES 4

🍂 Instead of dipping tortillas in oil to soften them, I like to use chicken stock for less calories and better flavor.

EXOTIC FRESH FRUIT TART

With the bounty of fruits available here, a fresh fruit tart is a must on the dessert tray every day. I use a classic French almond cream and my own sweet dough recipe. And I use whichever local fruits are currently fresh: strawberries, raspberries, star fruit, mangos, and pineapple. I've given some suggestions for fruit choices, but you can really use whatever looks the best at the market. This tart is wonderful served with freshly whipped cream and raspberry sauce (page 184). — *T.G.*

SWEET DOUGH

3/4 cup unsalted butter, at room temperature
1/2 cup granulated sugar
1 egg yolk
1/2 teaspoon vanilla extract
1/4 teaspoon lemon extract
2 tablespoons heavy cream
2 cups cake flour
1/4 teaspoon salt

ALMOND CREAM

1/2 cup unsalted butter, at room temperature
1 cup confectioners' sugar
1 1/4 cups ground almond
3 tablespoons all-purpose flour
3/4 teaspoon almond extract
2 eggs

1 tablespoon confectioners' sugar
1 cup pastry cream (page 184)
1/2 pineapple, peeled, cored, and sliced
1/2 mango, peeled, seeded, and sliced
1 pint fresh raspberries
2 star fruit, peeled, seeded, and sliced
2 tablespoons apricot jam
1 tablespoon water

To prepare the dough, in a bowl, using an electric mixer on medium speed, cream together the butter and granulated sugar until fluffy. Add the egg yolk, vanilla and lemon extracts, and cream and mix until incorporated.

In another bowl, sift together the flour and salt. Add to the butter mixture and, using the mixer on low speed, mix until incorporated. Remove from the bowl, press into a thick square on a sheet of plastic wrap, enclose in the wrap, and refrigerate for 1 to 2 hours.

To prepare the almond cream, in a bowl, using the mixer on medium speed, cream together the butter, confectioners' sugar, and almond. Add the flour and beat until combined. Scrape down the sides of the bowl and add the extract and the eggs, one at a time, beating well after each addition. Mix for about 5 minutes to make sure everything is fully incorporated.

Preheat the oven to 350°. Spray an 8-inch fluted tart pan with a removable bottom with vegetable-oil cooking spray. Knead the dough on a floured work surface until it is pliable. Roll out to 1/4 inch thick and 10 inches in diameter and carefully transfer to the prepared pan. Press into the bottom and sides of the pan. Using a rolling pin, press down on the pan edges to trim off the excess dough. Refrigerate for about 20 minutes and line with aluminum foil. Bake for 12 minutes, until light golden brown. Let cool. Carefully remove the foil and fill with half of the almond cream. (The rest of the almond cream can be kept in the freezer for up to 2 months.)

Dust with confectioners' sugar and bake for 20 to 25 minutes, until light golden brown. Let cool. Unmold by removing the pan sides and sliding the tart onto a serving plate.

Spread the pastry cream on top of the almond cream and arrange the fruit on top.

Dilute the apricot jam with the water. Heat the jam slightly and brush lightly over the fruit.

SERVES 6 TO 8

WHITE CHOCOLATE–RASPBERRY SOUFFLÉ CAKE

I wanted to make a flourless cake, so I took a soufflé recipe, let it fall, and turned it over not knowing, of course, if it would even work. After lots of trial and error, it did. I filled it with fresh raspberries and white chocolate mousse. It's very rich and made for true white chocolate lovers. — T.G.

WHITE CHOCOLATE SOUFFLÉ

8 ounces white chocolate

8 eggs, separated

1 cup sugar

6 tablespoons milk

2 pints fresh raspberries

3 cups white chocolate mousse (page 184)

WHITE CHOCOLATE RIBBON

4 ounces white chocolate

1 cup raspberry sauce (page 184)

Preheat the oven to 350°. Butter an 8 by 3-inch round cake pan. Line the bottom with parchment paper and butter the paper. Dust the paper and sides with sugar.

To make the soufflé, in the top pan of a double boiler, melt the chocolate over barely simmering water. Stir until smooth.

In a bowl, whisk together the yolks and $1/4$ cup of the sugar until pale yellow. In a saucepan, heat the milk over medium heat until small bubbles appear along the pan sides. Add the milk to the melted chocolate and stir to combine. Whisk the yolks into the chocolate mixture.

In a bowl, using an electric mixer on medium speed, beat the egg whites until soft peaks form. Increase the speed to high, add the remaining $3/4$ cup sugar, and beat until stiff peaks form. Fold the whites into the chocolate mixture in 2 batches.

Pour the batter into the prepared pan. Bake for 40 minutes, until golden brown. Remove from the oven and immediately invert onto a serving plate. Let cool completely. This *is* a soufflé. It *will* fall when you take it out of the oven.

Fill the center of the cake with the raspberries. Cover the top and sides of the cake with white chocolate mousse. Cover and refrigerate for 4 to 5 hours.

To prepare the ribbon, cut a piece of waxed paper to 3 by 26 inches. Melt the chocolate as you did for the cake and spread it onto the waxed paper with a bent palette knife. Place the sheet in the refrigerator for 5 minutes, until the chocolate begins to set. Remove from the refrigerator and, when the chocolate is pliable, drape the chocolate-coated waxed paper around the outside of the cake, with the chocolate side against the cake. This drape need not be perfect; you're going for a "crinkled" look. Refrigerate for 10 to 15 minutes, until the chocolate is hard. Carefully peel away the waxed paper.

Serve the cake with the raspberry sauce.

SERVES 8

FROZEN LEMONGRASS CRÈME BRÛLÉE
IN A GINGER PHYLLO TULIP

*This dessert was "born" at Avalon, in Northern California, when I worked for my friend Mark Ellman.
I wanted a different twist on crème brûlée, so it would be almost like an ice cream. It went over well.
I included the lemongrass in the crème brûlée because most of Mark's food was Thai influenced. When
I came back to Hali'imaile General Store, I brought the dessert with me.—T.G.*

CRÈME BRÛLÉE MIX

3 cups heavy cream

3/4 cup granulated sugar

2 lemongrass stalks, white part only, pounded

1 vanilla bean, split lengthwise

9 egg yolks

GINGER PHYLLO TULIP

3 tablespoons granulated sugar

1/2 teaspoon ground ginger

6 phyllo sheets

1/4 cup unsalted butter, melted

3/4 cup raw sugar

*1 pint fresh raspberries, blackberries,
    or strawberries*

To prepare the crème brûlée mix, in a saucepan, combine the cream, sugar, and lemongrass. Using the tip of a sharp knife, scrape the seeds from the vanilla bean into the pan, then add the pods. Bring to a boil over medium heat, stirring to dissolve the sugar, and remove from the heat. Remove the lemongrass and vanilla pods. Slowly ladle the cream mixture into the egg yolks, while whisking constantly. Return to the saucepan and continue to cook over low heat, stirring often, for 5 minutes, until the mixture has the consistency of a thick cream. Be careful not to overcook, or the yolks will scramble.

Strain through a fine-mesh sieve into a clean bowl and cool down by nesting over a bowl of ice.

Line 6 standard muffin-tin cups with plastic wrap. Pour the cooled custard into the muffin cups and freeze.

Preheat the oven to 350°.

To prepare the phyllo tulip, in a small bowl, mix together the sugar and ginger. Roll one sheet of dough out flat, keeping the others covered. Brush the sheet with the melted butter and sprinkle with 1/2 teaspoon of the sugar mixture. Repeat with the remaining pieces of dough, stacking each on top of the last. Cut the dough stack into 6 equal rectangles.

Invert a large muffin tin on a work surface. Spray with vegetable-oil cooking spray. Mold each section of phyllo dough over 1 of the muffin molds. Make sure they are not touching.

Bake for about 15 minutes, until golden brown. Remove from the oven and carefully pull the phyllo "tulips" from the muffin molds immediately. Place on a rack to cool for 30 minutes.

Remove the custards from the freezer. Holding the plastic wrap, lift each custard out of the muffin cups, then peel off the plastic. When ready to serve, spread the top of each custard with 2 tablespoons of the raw sugar. Using a butane torch, caramelize

the sugar. Alternatively, place the custards on a baking sheet and slip under a hot broiler just long enough to caramelize the sugar. Watch closely as they burn easily.

With a small metal spatula, pop each custard into a phyllo tulip. Serve with the fresh berries.

SERVES 6

MANGO-PINEAPPLE COBBLER

It's a traditional cobbler with "crumb and crust" — again using two of Hawai'i's signature fruits — and is one of the easiest and most delicious desserts to make. — T.G.

1 recipe sweet dough (page 78)

CRUMB

1 cup firmly packed brown sugar
1¹/₂ cups flour
1 tablespoon ground cinnamon
¹/₂ cup unsalted butter, cold

FRUIT FILLING I

4 mangos (about 2 pounds), peeled, pitted, and chopped
1¹/₂ cups granulated sugar
¹/₃ cup cornstarch

FRUIT FILLING II

1 large or 1¹/₂ small pineapples (about 2 pounds), peeled and chopped
1¹/₂ cups firmly packed brown sugar
¹/₃ cup cornstarch

2 tablespoons granulated sugar
¹/₂ teaspoon ground nutmeg
Vanilla ice cream, for serving

On a floured work surface, roll out the dough to ¹/₄ inch thick and cut out 18 fluted rounds, each 1¹/₂ inches in diameter, for the top of the cobblers. Refrigerate until ready to assemble the cobblers.

To prepare the crumb, in a bowl, stir together the brown sugar, flour, and cinnamon. Add the butter and cut in with a pastry blender until the mixture has the consistency of fine meal. (Alternatively, mix the dry ingredients in a food processor, then add the butter and pulse until you get a fine crumb. No big lumps of butter, please!)

To prepare filling I, in a bowl, combine all the ingredients and mix well. Prepare filling II the same way in a separate bowl.

Preheat the oven to 325°.

Divide the pineapple filling evenly among 6 (10-ounce) individual soufflé dishes. Top with the mango filling, dividing evenly. Then evenly divide the crumb among the dishes, sprinkling it on top of the mango.

Combine the sugar and nutmeg in a small bowl and mix well. Remove the dough rounds from the refrigerator and place 3 on top of each crumb topping (which, by this time, is looking much too full, but don't be alarmed, it shrinks quite a bit). Brush with water and sprinkle with the nutmeg sugar. Bake for 1¹/₄ hours, until the cobbler starts to bubble. Let cool slightly before serving. Accompany each serving with a scoop of vanilla ice cream.

SERVES 6

✤ If you can't find fresh mangos, frozen ones will work just fine. Thaw them halfway before mixing.

MACADAMIA NUT LACE TULIP FILLED WITH ASSORTED TROPICAL SORBETS

This is a French recipe that I adapted, incorporating macadamia nuts in place of almonds. It's beautiful and refreshing for a hot day—another easy-to-make and charming-to-serve dessert.—T.G.

MACADAMIA NUT LACE COOKIES

1/2 cup whole macadamia nuts, chopped into medium-sized pieces

2/3 cup sugar

1/3 cup flour

Finely chopped zest and juice from 1 large orange

5 tablespoons unsalted butter, melted

Assorted sorbets of your choice

1 cup raspberry sauce (page 184), for garnish

Preheat the oven to 325°.

To prepare the cookies, in a bowl, mix together the macadamia nuts, sugar, and flour. Add the orange zest and juice and the butter and mix well. Cover and refrigerate for about 1 hour, until hardened.

Line a baking sheet with parchment paper and spray the paper with vegetable-oil cooking spray. Using a 1/4-cup scoop, place 6 scoops of the dough as far apart as possible on the prepared baking sheet. Wet your hands and pat the balls down slightly to flatten the balls to 1/4 inch tall and 2 inches in diameter.

Bake for 15 to 20 minutes, until a light golden brown. Remove from the oven and let sit on the baking sheet until not too hot to handle but warm enough to still be pliable.

Mold the warm cookies around the bowls of 6 wineglasses so they resemble tulips. If the cookies feel too hard, just pop them back in the oven until they are pliable again. Let stand until they harden and cool completely, then slip off of the glasses.

Fill each cookie with your favorite sorbet. Garnish the plates with raspberry sauce. The tulips look especially nice when you use two or three different sorbet flavors.

SERVES 6

THE CRAB DIP, THE CRAB DIP . . . HMM. SHALL I PUT IT HERE?
NO, I DON'T THINK IT REALLY BELONGS IN SUMMER.

Fall Recipes to Excite the Senses

I met Tom in 1984, while planning the opening party for his wife's new advertising agency. We found that we were actually neighbors and soon became fast friends. "Party Animal Tom" had spontaneous ceramic-firing parties at his house, and it became a custom for me to bring the food. Joe and I were the starving artist collectors: we wanted Tom's art, and he needed to eat. Some time later, Tom began working with molten metals, and I longed for a nine-foot-high bronze bas relief of an island woman that I saw at his studio. It was the first piece of art we bought for the store. That purchase led to commissioning Tom to make a matching bar top. Years later he made the bar for our second restaurant, Joe's Bar & Grill. ❧

Cathy Gannon mixing mai tais at Tom's bar.

BLACKENED SASHIMI
WITH "COOL" POTATO SALAD

This was the first raw-fish appetizer that we put on the menu, pre-1990, my twist on the East meets West craze. The combination of potato salad and raw fish came as a surprise to our customers, but it quickly turned into a favorite.

"COOL" POTATO SALAD

1 teaspoon salt

4 cups peeled and cubed potatoes

1/2 cup good-quality mayonnaise

1/4 cup sour cream

2 tablespoons chopped fresh basil

2 tablespoons chopped fresh chives

2 tablespoons chopped fresh dill

1/4 cup capers, drained

1/4 teaspoon salt

Pinch of white pepper

SEASONING MIX

1 tablespoon cayenne pepper

1 tablespoon freshly ground black pepper

1 tablespoon paprika

1 teaspoon dried thyme leaves

1 teaspoon dried oregano leaves

2 teaspoons garlic powder

2 teaspoons onion powder

2 1/2 teaspoons salt

*1 pound sashimi-grade ahi (yellowfin) or any
     good-grade tuna*

1/2 cup unsalted butter, melted and cooled

To prepare the potato salad, in a saucepan, add the salt and potatoes and water to cover. Cover, bring to a boil, and cook for about 10 minutes, until the potatoes are just fork tender. Drain and set aside to cool.

In a large bowl, combine the mayonnaise and sour cream. Add the basil, chives, dill, and capers and mix well. Add the potatoes and mix well. Season with salt and pepper. Cover and chill well.

To prepare the seasoning mix, combine all the ingredients and mix well. (You can substitute a premixed Cajun spice blend for this mixture.) Spread on a plate.

Heat a cast-iron skillet over high heat until the pan stops smoking and ash has collected on the pan bottom. This will take 10 to 15 minutes.

Cut the fish into 2 by 2 by 6-inch blocks. Dip the fish in the melted butter and coat with the spice mix. Place in the skillet and sear on each side for 30 to 45 seconds, until blackened, but still rare inside. Transfer to a plate and allow to cool. Slice very thinly across the grain with a very sharp knife.

To serve, place a spoonful of the potato salad in the center of each plate. Fan 3 or 4 slices of fish around each plate and serve immediately.

SERVES 8

🍃 This dish must be prepared either outdoors or in a well-ventilated kitchen. And note that the fish must be seared in a cast-iron skillet. A word about these great pans: make the investment because they are truly indestructible. And they make great "frahd" chicken!

GOAT CHEESE AND MAUI ONION TART
WITH SMOKED TOMATO COULIS

I started out making this tart with leeks, but then I changed the recipe to include caramelized Maui onions instead, to give it more island flavor. Basically, I'm a fan of savory cheesecakes. It's another one of those dishes that was on our menu for years, and we created an uproar with our customers every time we tried to take it off. This tart is especially tasty garnished with fried onion rings.

1 pound cream cheese, at room temperature

1/2 pound fresh goat cheese, at room temperature

4 eggs

1/2 cup heavy cream

2 teaspoons ground nutmeg

2 tablespoons chopped fresh chives

1 teaspoon salt

1/2 teaspoon freshly ground black pepper

1 tablespoon unsalted butter

1 large Maui onion, thinly sliced

1 prebaked savory 10-inch tart shell

6 tomatoes (about 3 pounds), seeded and peeled

To prepare the filling, in a food processor, combine the cream cheese and goat cheese and pulse until smooth. Add the eggs, one at a time, pulsing after each addition. Add the cream, nutmeg, chives, salt, and pepper and pulse to blend.

In a sauté pan, melt the butter over medium heat. Add the onion and cook, stirring occasionally, for about 15 minutes, until caramelized. Remove from the heat and allow to cool. Meanwhile, preheat the oven to 350°.

Spread the onions evenly in the bottom of the tart shell. Pour the cheese mixture over the onions. Bake for about 45 minutes, until set in the center. Allow to cool.

To prepare the coulis, quarter the tomatoes lengthwise and place in the basket of a pasta pot. Cover the bottom of the pot with 2 cups mesquite wood chips. Place the basket in the pot and cover the pot with aluminum foil. Punch holes in the foil. Set the pot over medium heat and smoke for 10 minutes. Turn off the heat and allow to sit, covered, for 10 minutes longer. Transfer the tomatoes to a food processor or blender and purée. Place the purée in saucepan over medium heat and reduce, stirring occasionally, for about 15 minutes, until thick. Season with salt and pepper.

Cut the tart into 8 wedges and place on individual plates. Using a ladle, spoon the sauce on each plate and top with a wedge of tart.

SERVES 8

BLACK BEAN SOUP

The first time I ever tasted black bean soup was in a hole-in-the-wall Cuban restaurant in New York City. The soup came to the table with lots of side garnishes, of which my favorite was the fried plantains. Since bananas of all varieties are so plentiful here on the Islands, they became the garnish on my version of that original taste treat.

2 cups dried black beans

2¹/2 quarts water

4 tablespoons unsalted butter

2 celery stalks, chopped

1 large onion, chopped

6 cups vegetable stock, plus extra for thinning, if needed (see page 10)

1 ham hock

1 lemongrass stalk, white part only, pounded

1 clove garlic, unpeeled

Freshly ground black pepper

Salt

3 teaspoons ground cumin

¹/4 cup chopped fresh parsley

Sour cream, for garnish

6 sprigs cilantro, for garnish

6 avocado slices, for garnish

6 banana slices, cut on the diagonal, for garnish

Rinse and pick over the beans. Place the beans in a saucepan, add water to cover, and bring to a boil. Allow to boil for 5 minutes, uncovered, then remove from the heat. Let stand for 1 hour and then drain.

In a large soup pot, combine the beans with the 2¹/2 quarts water. Bring to a boil over high heat, decrease the heat to low, and simmer, uncovered, for about 1¹/2 hours, until the beans are tender to the bite.

In a large, deep skillet, melt the butter over medium heat. Add the celery and onion and sauté for 5 minutes, until limp. Do not brown. Add the beans with their liquid, stock, ham hock, lemongrass, garlic, and pepper to taste. Simmer for 3 to 4 hours, until the flavor of the soup ripens.

Remove the ham hock, lemongrass, and garlic. Drain the beans through a sieve, reserving the broth in a saucepan. In a blender or food processor, purée the beans, then pour into the saucepan with the broth. Add the salt, cumin, and parsley and simmer over medium heat for at least 5 minutes, until heated through. Add more salt if needed, and additional vegetable stock if the soup is too thick.

Ladle into warmed soup bowls and garnish each serving with sour cream, a cilantro sprig, an avocado slice, and a banana slice.

SERVES 6

✤ If you don't want to spend time cooking and soaking the black beans, here's a shortcut. Start with a good commercial brand of canned black beans, rinse them, heat them with chicken stock, and then continue on with the recipe.

Clam Chowder

I bet I've put fifty thousand pounds of clams into soup pots over the last dozen years. It's one of those soups everyone loves to see on the menu. I prefer mine not too thick, and it's much better the day after you make it.

6 slices bacon, diced

1 onion, chopped

2 celery stalks, thinly sliced

4 cloves garlic, minced

4 potatoes, peeled and cut into $^1\!/_2$-inch cubes

4 cups bottled clam juice

4 cups chopped clams, preferably frozen
    and thawed

1 tablespoon Worcestershire sauce

1 teaspoon Tabasco sauce

2 cups heavy cream

1 teaspoon salt

$^1\!/_2$ teaspoon white pepper

2 tablespoons chopped fresh chives, for garnish

In a large saucepan, sauté the bacon over medium heat until crisp. Add the onion, celery, and garlic and sauté for 2 minutes, until the onions are translucent. Add the potatoes and clam juice and simmer for about 20 minutes, until the potatoes are tender. Add the clams, Worcestershire sauce, Tabasco, and cream and simmer just until heated through. Season with salt and pepper. Ladle into warmed bowls and garnish with the chives. Serve at once.

Serves 6

ROASTED RED PEPPER SOUP

The only way I personally like red bell peppers is if they're roasted. When we first opened, "simple" was very important, and this is simple. You can throw it together in less than a half hour. You can serve this to your strict vegetarian friends by substituting vegetable stock for chicken stock.

1 tablespoon olive oil

4 tablespoons unsalted butter

3 cloves garlic, chopped

1 large onion, chopped

3 shallots, coarsely chopped

8 red bell peppers, roasted (see note)

4 cups rich chicken stock (see page 10)

Pinch of cayenne pepper

Salt

Freshly ground black pepper

CILANTRO-LIME CREAM

1/2 cup sour cream

Juice of 1 lime

2 tablespoons chopped fresh cilantro, plus extra for garnish

In a saucepan, heat the oil and butter over medium heat. Add the garlic, onion, and shallots and sauté for 2 minutes, until limp. Add the peppers and cook for 6 to 8 minutes, until softened. Add the stock, cayenne pepper, salt, and pepper. Bring to a boil, decrease the heat to low, cover, and simmer for 25 minutes, until the peppers are beginning to fall apart.

Pour the soup through a sieve, reserving the liquid. Place the solids into a food processor or blender and purée until smooth. Return to the saucepan with the reserved liquid, stir well, and heat through over medium heat.

To prepare the cream, in a bowl, combine all the ingredients and mix well. Ladle the soup into warmed bowls and garnish with the cream and cilantro.

SERVES 8

To ROAST BELL PEPPERS, place them directly on a gas flame or under a preheated broiler, rotating them until they are completely charred. Place them in a brown paper bag, close tightly, and allow to sweat for 5 minutes. Peel off the blackened skin. Remove the stems, slit open, and remove the seeds. Rinse briefly under cold running water. Drain on paper towels, then slice into long, wide strips.

WILD RICE SALAD

I made this up for our daughter Jana's wedding in 1995. It contains ingredients I love to use: pecans, which take me back to Texas, blue cheese, and grapes. The combo works deliciously. Add some julienned smoked chicken and you have a great main-course salad.

CITRUS-MISO VINAIGRETTE

1 tablespoon yellow miso

1 tablespoon freshly squeezed lemon juice

1 tablespoon freshly squeezed orange juice

1 1/2 tablespoons sherry

1/4 cup canola oil

1/4 cup chopped fresh cilantro

SALAD

2 cups cooked wild rice

1/4 cup pecan halves, toasted and coarsely chopped (page 106)

1/2 cup halved seedless Red Flame grapes

1/4 cup crumbled blue cheese

1/4 cup thinly sliced green onion, white and green parts

1/2 teaspoon salt

1/2 teaspoon black pepper

To prepare the vinaigrette, in a blender, combine the miso, lemon juice, orange juice, and sherry. Process to mix. With the motor running, drizzle in the oil until emulsified. Pour into a small bowl and stir in the cilantro with a spatula. (Extra dressing can be stored in an airtight container in the refrigerator for up to 1 week. It is a wonderful addition to any salad, and can also be used as a marinade for chicken and fish.)

To prepare the salad, in a bowl, toss together the rice, pecans, grapes, cheese, and green onion. Season with salt and pepper. Drizzle with the vinaigrette to desired taste and toss well. Serve immediately.

SERVES 4

🌿 Whenever you cook rice—any kind of rice—cook it in stock or juice, not water, to get a more flavorful result.

GRILLED SHIITAKE MUSHROOM, ROASTED PEPPER, AND FRESH MOZZARELLA SALAD

A simple, flavorful salad that combines great Asian and Italian flavors. I use more shiitake mushrooms than any other mushroom. It seems to be the all-purpose mushroom of Hawai'i Regional Cuisine. When grilled, it has a rich deep flavor and firm texture.

DRESSING

1/4 cup extra virgin olive oil

1 teaspoon Asian sesame oil

2 cloves garlic, minced

1 tablespoon ginger, minced

1/2 teaspoon freshly ground black pepper

8 large shiitake mushrooms

2 tablespoons extra virgin olive oil

1 red bell pepper, roasted (page 97)

1 yellow bell pepper, roasted (page 97)

1/2 pound fresh mozzarella cheese, sliced

4 fresh basil leaves

Prepare a fire in a charcoal grill, or preheat a gas grill.

To prepare the dressing, in a small skillet, heat the oils, garlic, ginger, and pepper together over medium heat for about 1 minute to infuse the oils with the seasonings. Do not allow the garlic and ginger to brown. Pour through a fine-mesh sieve and allow to cool.

Brush the mushrooms with the oil, place on the grill rack, and grill, turning once, for 2 to 3 minutes on each side, until lightly browned and marked by the grill.

Cut the peppers into long 1/4-inch-wide strips. Place the mushrooms, peppers, mozzarella, and basil on a plate and drizzle with the dressing. Serve at once.

SERVES 4

If you don't want to take the time—or don't have the time—to roast and peel bell peppers, you can use a good-quality bottled brand, but be sure to rinse them to remove the canned taste and dry them well.

WARM GOAT CHEESE CREPE AND DUCK SALAD

I am a big fan of duck. It has much more flavor than chicken, and once you learn how to cook it properly, you will find it almost as versatile. This was the first duck appetizer I ever put on the menu. Since then, we've always had one, in one form or another.

CHIVE CREPES

1/4 cup plus 1 tablespoon flour

Pinch of salt

1 egg

1/4 cup plus 2 tablespoons milk

2 tablespoons clarified butter, melted (page 167)

2 teaspoons chopped fresh chives

1 (5-pound) duck

Salt

Freshly ground black pepper

RASPBERRY VINAIGRETTE

1/4 cup olive oil

2 tablespoons raspberry vinegar

1 teaspoon crème fraîche (page 60)

2 tablespoons fresh raspberries

1 teaspoon salt

Pinch of white pepper

1 (1/2-pound) log fresh goat cheese, cut into 8 equal rounds

6 cups mesclun

2 cups arugula, torn

1 (15-ounce) can hearts of palm, drained and cut into 1 inch slices

2 heads endive, chopped, with 8 whole leaves reserved for garnish

8 teaspoons macadamia nut pieces, toasted (page 106), for garnish

To prepare the crepes, in a bowl, combine the flour and salt. Add the egg and whisk well. Slowly whisk in the milk. Strain through a fine-mesh sieve into a clean bowl, cover, and refrigerate for about 2 hours. Just before you're ready to cook, add 1 tablespoon of the clarified butter and the chives to the batter and stir well.

To prepare the duck, preheat the oven to 400°. Prick the duck skin all over with a sharp knife. Season the duck with salt and pepper. Place the duck, skin side up, on a rack in a roasting pan. Roast for 30 minutes. Decrease the heat to 350° and roast, basting frequently, for 1 hour longer, until the skin is brown and crisp. The meat is done when the juices run clear after a thigh is pierced. Allow to cool.

Remove the skin from the duck and place the skin in a saucepan with 2 tablespoons of the drippings from the roasting pan. Cook over low heat for 12 to 15 minutes, until all the fat is rendered. Using a slotted spoon, transfer the cracklings to paper towels to drain. Remove the meat from the bones and julienne. Cover and set aside.

To cook the crepes, heat a 6-inch nonstick sauté pan over medium-high heat until the pan is very hot. Reduce the heat to medium. Brush the pan with a little of the clarified butter. When it sizzles, add 1 tablespoon of the batter. Swirl the batter in the pan to form a thin sheet. Cook for 35 to 45 seconds, until the first side is set. Turn the crepe over and cook for another 6 seconds. Flip onto a plate. Repeat with the remaining batter, brushing a little more butter in the pan after every second or third crepe. You should have around 10 crepes in all.

To prepare the vinaigrette, in a blender, combine the oil, vinegar, crème fraîche, and raspberries. Process until smooth. Season with salt and pepper.

Place a cheese round on each crepe and fold in all 4 sides to form a rectangular package. Heat the crepes in the microwave for about 45 seconds, until the cheese melts and the crepes are hot, or warm in a preheated 350° oven for about 5 minutes.

To assemble the salad, in a large bowl, toss together the mesclun, arugula, hearts of palm, and chopped endive. Add the dressing and toss to coat evenly.

To assemble the salads, divide the greens among 8 plates. Top each salad with a warm crepe and one-eighth of the duck meat. Garnish with the cracklings, endive leaves, and macadamia nuts. Serve immediately.

SERVES 8

🐝 Always use a nonstick pan to make crepes. Forget those fancy steel crepe pans that need to be seasoned.

COCONUT SEAFOOD CURRY

Curry has always been one of my favorite things to make. Every time we do an Asian-themed party, we prepare a big curry table with bowls of condiments and a lamb curry, a vegetable curry, and a seafood curry. The presentation is beautiful. It was a natural to put a curry dish on the store menu. It's also a great way to use all those succulent fish collar and tail pieces. Plus, no one who orders fish has to get an end piece!

JASMINE-LEMONGRASS RICE

1 cup jasmine rice

1 cup plus 1 tablespoon water

$^1/_2$ lemongrass stalk, cut in half lengthwise
    and pounded

2 tablespoons olive oil

2 tablespoons julienned onion

1 pound peeled and deveined shrimp

$^1/_2$ pound firm fish fillets, cut into 1-inch cubes

$^1/_4$ cup julienned red bell pepper

$^1/_2$ cup sliced shiitake mushrooms

$^1/_2$ cup sugar snap peas or snow peas

1 tablespoon green Thai curry paste

2 cups frozen coconut milk, thawed

Toasted shredded dried coconut, for garnish

Dry-roasted peanuts, for garnish

To prepare the rice, place it in a sieve and rinse under cold running water until the water runs clear. Drain well, place in a rice cooker, and add the water and lemongrass. Cover and cook, until the timer goes off, then let the rice stand for 10 minutes before removing lid. Remove and discard the lemongrass.

If you don't have a rice cooker, go out and buy one! Or, you can put the rice, water, and lemongrass into a saucepan, bring to a simmer, cover, reduce the heat to low, and cook for 15 to 20 minutes, until the rice is tender and the liquid absorbed. Remove from the heat, let stand for 15 minutes, then remove and discard the lemongrass.

To prepare the curry, in a large sauté pan, heat 1 tablespoon of the oil over medium heat. Add the onion and sauté for 3 minutes, until softened. Add the shrimp and sauté for 2 to 3 minutes, until they just begin to curl and turn pink. Transfer to a plate and keep warm. Add the fish and sauté for 3 minutes, until cooked through. Transfer to the plate with the shrimp. Heat the remaining 1 tablespoon oil, add the bell pepper, and sauté for 2 minutes, until softened. Add the mushrooms and sauté for 1 minute, then add the peas and sauté for 1 minute longer, until fork tender. Add the curry paste and stir to coat the vegetables. Cook for 1 minute, until incorporated into the mixture. Add the coconut milk and, stirring constantly, cook for 2 minutes, until hot. Add the reserved shrimp and fish and cook until heated through.

To serve, ladle the curry over the rice and garnish with the coconut and peanuts.

SERVES 4

Thai curry paste is available in yellow, green, and red. Red is the hottest, so use whichever suits your taste.

Opakapaka with Lobster and Shrimp
Baked in Parchment with Asian Butter

My favorite thing about this dish is watching the smiles that appear on our guests' faces at the first whiff as their server cuts open the parchment.

ASIAN BUTTER

¹/₂ cup unsalted butter, at room temperature

1¹/₂ teaspoons soy sauce

¹/₂ teaspoon minced garlic

¹/₂ teaspoon Asian sesame oil

¹/₄ teaspoon Vietnamese garlic-chile sauce

1 tablespoon minced fresh cilantro

1 carrot, peeled and julienned

2 leeks, white part only, split and thinly sliced

¹/₄ cup sliced green onion, green part only

2 tablespoons peeled and minced fresh ginger

1 pound opakapaka fillet, cut into 4 equal portions

4 large shrimp, peeled and deveined

Meat from 4 lobster claws

¹/₂ cup sliced shiitake mushrooms

Salt

Freshly ground black pepper

To prepare the butter, in a bowl, combine all the ingredients and mix well. Place the seasoned butter on a piece of plastic wrap and roll into a log. Place in the refrigerator until ready to use.

Preheat the oven to 375°.

Cut out 4 pieces of parchment paper 20 inches wide by 12 inches long. Fold each in half lengthwise to form 10 by 12-inch rectangles. Cut each into a half-heart shape from the fold to form a full heart when unfolded. Unfold the hearts and place one-eighth of the carrot, leek, green onion, and ginger in the center of one side. Place 1 piece of fish on each bed of vegetables. Top the fish with the shrimp, lobster meat, the rest of the vegetables, and the mushrooms. Season with salt and pepper. Dot each fillet with 2 tablespoons of the Asian butter. Fold the uncovered side of the heart over to cover the fish and crease the edges together to seal the package.

Place the packages on a baking sheet and bake for 10 to 12 minutes. To test for doneness, open the corner of a package and pierce the fish and vegetables with a fork. Transfer to individual plates and let each diner snip open his or her package.

SERVES 4

You can purchase parchment paper at any kitchen-supply store like Williams-Sonoma or Executive Chef, or at well-stocked supermarkets. Aluminum foil can be substituted.

Kula Vegetable Torte

A sentimental favorite. I prepared it for Great Chefs of Hawai'i, the Discovery Channel series, which also resulted in a cookbook. I learned early on—once we got our bearings that we were a restaurant!— that you had to have a hearty vegetable dish on the menu in addition to the BLTs and the Reubens. It was on the menu for years from within a few months of opening.

2½ (10 by 15½-inch) sheets frozen puff pastry

2 cups broccoli florets

2 cups green beans, cut into ½-inch pieces

3 tablespoons olive oil

2 cups peeled and sliced carrot

¼ cup peeled and minced fresh ginger

2 cups thinly sliced onion

2 tablespoons sesame seeds, toasted (page 63)

2 cloves garlic, minced

3 eggs, beaten

2 cups (1 pound) ricotta cheese

2 tablespoons minced fresh cilantro

2 teaspoons salt

1 teaspoon freshly ground black pepper

2 red bell peppers, roasted (page 97)

1 egg white, beaten

2 tablespoons poppy seeds

Herbed Yogurt Sauce

2 cups plain yogurt

1 tablespoon chopped fresh dill

1 tablespoon chopped fresh cilantro

2 teaspoons minced garlic

2 tablespoons freshly squeezed lime juice

Place the puff pastry in the refrigerator to thaw overnight.

To prepare the vegetables, bring a saucepan of salted water to a boil. Add the broccoli and blanch for 2 minutes. Remove from the pan with a wire skimmer and plunge into a bowl of ice water to stop the cooking. Drain again and set aside in a bowl.

Add the green beans to the same saucepan of boiling water and parboil for 2 minutes, until al dente. Drain and plunge into a bowl of ice water to stop the cooking. Drain again and set aside in a separate bowl.

In a sauté pan or skillet, heat 2 tablespoons of the oil over medium heat. Add the carrot and sauté for 3 to 4 minutes, until barely tender. Transfer to a bowl, stir in the ginger, and set aside.

In the same pan, heat the remaining 1 tablespoon oil over medium heat. Add the onion and sauté for 2 minutes, until translucent. Remove from the heat.

Drain any liquid from the vegetables and blot them all with paper towels. Toss the broccoli with the sesame seeds. Toss the green beans with the garlic. In yet another bowl, combine the eggs, ricotta, cilantro, salt, and pepper and mix well.

Spray a 10-inch springform pan with vegetable-oil cooking spray. Cut 1 sheet of the puff pastry in half lengthwise. Use one-half of the sheet to cover half of the inside rim of the prepared pan, leaving 1 inch overlapping the top edge of the pan. Gently tuck the bottom edge into the corner of the pan. Repeat with the other half-sheet of dough so that the inside rim of the pan is completely lined. Gently pinch the edges of the pastry together where they meet. Set the pan on the remaining whole puff pastry sheet and carefully cut around the outside edge to make a circle of pastry. Place the pastry circle into the bottom of the pan and press into the corners to seal. Make 1 layer of each of the following in the lined pan: carrot, onion, green beans, ricotta cheese mixture, broccoli, and peppers. As it is added, press each layer firmly into the pan.

Cut ¼-inch-wide strips from the remaining half sheet of

puff pastry. Using the strips, make a lattice design to cover the top of the torte. Gently fold the overlapping edges of dough over the top of the torte. With a pastry brush, glaze the entire top with the egg white. Sprinkle with the poppy seeds. Cover and refrigerate the torte for 45 minutes.

Preheat the oven to 425°. Bake the torte for 50 minutes, until well browned. Remove from the oven and allow to cool on a rack for 2 to 3 hours.

To prepare the sauce, in a bowl, stir together all the ingredients until well combined.

Release the pan sides and slide the torte onto a serving plate. Cut into 8 wedges and place each on a plate. Drizzle 1/4 cup of the yogurt sauce over the top of each slice and onto the plate.

SERVES 8

GRILLED SHUTOME OVER PASTA FORIANA

The pasta portion of this dish is made with an unusual combination of ingredients. Don't let that discourage you from making it. The blending of all these flavors really works to create a delicious sauce. I had some customers who ordered a big portion to go every week, regardless of whether or not it was on the menu.

1 cup extra virgin olive oil

12 anchovy fillets, chopped

4 cloves garlic, chopped

1/2 cup walnut pieces, toasted (see note)

4 tablespoons pine nuts, toasted (see note)

1/2 cup raisins

1 teaspoon dried oregano

2 pinches of crushed red pepper flakes

1/2 pound spaghetti

*2 tablespoons chopped fresh flat-leaf parsley,
    plus 2 tablespoons for garnish*

4 (5-ounce) shutome (swordfish) fillets

Prepare a fire in a charcoal grill, or preheat a gas grill.

In a small sauté pan, heat 2 tablespoons of the olive oil over low heat. Add the anchovies and cook for 1 minute, until they begin to break down. Stir in the garlic and cook for 1 minute, until softened. Add the walnut pieces, pine nuts, raisins, oregano, and pepper flakes and sauté for 1 minute longer to warm the ingredients. Stir in the remaining olive oil, set aside, and keep warm.

Bring a large pot filled with salted water to a boil. Add the spaghetti, stir well, and cook for about 10 minutes, until al dente. Drain the pasta, add to the pan with the sauce, add the parsley, and toss to coat. Meanwhile, place the fish fillets on the grill rack and grill, turning once, for 4 minutes on each side, for medium well.

Divide the pasta among warmed individual plates, top with the fish, and garnish with the parsley. Serve immediately.

SERVES 4

🌿 To TOAST NUTS, preheat the oven to 375°. Spread the nuts out on a baking sheet. Bake until the nuts take on a slightly darker color, the timing will vary depending on the size. I'd suggest you start with 5 minutes, but check the nuts frequently as they can burn easily.

PORTUGUESE SAUSAGE AND CLAMS

I demonstrated this dish on Northwest Afternoon, *a Seattle-based television show that did a week of broadcasts from Maui. Truth be told, I created this recipe because I had some beautiful bowls that cried out for something colorful to fill them. As unusual as it sounds, clams and sausage go well together. If you have some homemade fish stock in the freezer, this is a quick, easy, and delicious one-pot dinner.*

1/3 cup olive oil

1 tablespoon finely chopped garlic

1 tablespoon peeled and finely chopped fresh ginger

2 cups chopped onion

3 cups chopped red bell pepper

1/2 pound mild Portuguese sausage (linguiça), cut into 1/4-inch chunks

1 1/2 cups sake

6 cups rich fish stock (see page 10) or bottled clam juice

1 tablespoon Vietnamese garlic-chile sauce

2 cups peeled, seeded, and coarsely chopped tomato

5 dozen clams, well scrubbed

1/2 cup chopped fresh cilantro, for garnish

In a large sauté pan, heat the oil over medium heat. Add the garlic, ginger, onion, and bell peppers and sauté for 2 minutes, until wilted. Add the sausage and sauté for another 5 minutes, until the sausage is lightly browned. Add the sake to the mixture and deglaze the pan, stirring to dislodge any browned bits on the pan bottom. Add the fish stock and cook for 10 minutes, until reduced by half. Add the chile sauce and the tomato and stir well.

Discard any clams that fail to close to the touch and add the remaining ones to the pan. Cover and cook for 6 to 8 minutes, until the clams open. Discard any clams that fail to open. Ladle into warmed bowls and garnish with the cilantro. Serve immediately.

SERVES 6

PUMPKIN SEED–CRUSTED SCALLOPS WITH ROASTED VEGETABLE ENCHILADAS

A menu item created for the start of the new millennium, the availability of large fresh sea scallops allowed us to invent this instant hit. If you're lucky enough to find fresh diver scallops, which are harvested by hand, use them for this dish. We have had enchiladas on our dinner menu for years, so using the vegetable enchiladas as an accompaniment to this dish worked perfectly.

TOMATILLO CREAM SAUCE

1 tablespoon olive oil

1 onion, chopped

2 cloves garlic, minced

1 cup peeled and chopped fresh tomatillos

1 tablespoon chipotle chile in adobo

2 cups chicken stock (see page 10)

1 cup heavy cream

2 teaspoons ground cumin

1 tablespoon freshly squeezed lime juice

Salt

White pepper

ROASTED VEGETABLE ENCHILADAS

1 onion, coarsely chopped

1 globe eggplant, coarsely chopped

1 zucchini, coarsely chopped

1 yellow squash, coarsely chopped

1 yellow bell pepper, seeded and coarsely chopped

1 tablespoon fresh lemon thyme, chopped

3 tablespoons extra virgin olive oil

Salt

Freshly ground black pepper

6 corn tortillas

1 cup chicken stock, heated (see page 10)

CHIPOTLE HONEY BUTTER

1/2 cup dry white wine

2 teaspoons honey

1/4 cup heavy cream

1 teaspoon minced chipotle chile in adobo

3/4 cup cold unsalted butter, cut into pieces

1 cup pepitas (toasted pumpkin seeds)

3 cups panko (Japanese bread crumbs)

1/4 cup chopped fresh dill

3 egg whites

24 large sea scallops

1/4 cup clarified butter (page 167)

To prepare the sauce, in a saucepan, heat the oil over medium-high heat. Add the onion and garlic and sauté for 4 minutes, until softened. Add the tomatillos, chile, and chicken stock and bring to a boil. Decrease the heat to low and simmer, uncovered, for 20 minutes, until the tomatillos break down. Add the cream and cook over low heat for 10 minutes, until reduced by half. With a hand blender, blend until smooth. Add the cumin, lime juice, and salt and white pepper to taste and mix well. Set aside.

To prepare the enchiladas, preheat the oven to 375°. In a roasting pan, toss all the vegetables with the thyme, oil, and salt and pepper to taste. Roast in the oven for about 10 minutes, until just tender.

Transfer the roasted vegetables to a food processor and pulse 2 or 3 times to achieve a medium dice. Reduce the oven temperature to 350°.

Dip a tortilla in the hot stock and place on a plate. Top with one-sixth of the vegetable mixture and roll up into a cylinder. Place seam side down in a baking dish. Repeat with the remaining tortillas and vegetables. Pour the tomatillo sauce over the enchiladas. Bake for 10 to 12 minutes, until the sauce is bubbling.

To prepare the butter, in a saucepan, combine the wine,

honey, cream, and chile over medium-high heat. Cook for about 8 minutes, until reduced by half. Whisk in the butter a piece at a time, until incorporated and smooth.

To prepare the coating, in a food processor, combine the *pepitas,* panko, and dill and pulse until a fine crumb mixture forms. Place in a shallow bowl. Place the egg whites in a separate shallow bowl and lightly whip until foamy. Dip the scallops in the egg whites and then roll in the crumb mixture to coat evenly.

In a heavy sauté pan, heat 2 tablespoons of the clarified butter over medium heat. Add half of the scallops, and cook, turning once, for about 2 minutes on each side, until browned and cooked through. Repeat with the remaining clarified butter and scallops.

To serve, place 4 scallops on each plate and top with the honey butter. Place an enchilada alongside and drizzle with the tomatillo sauce. Serve at once.

SERVES 6

LOBSTER RAGOUT WITH CORN CUSTARD

I created this recipe for a Big Island Bounty lunch that was presented by women chefs in the mid-1990s. I was responible for the entrée. It's a great looking dish with a fun presentation.

CORN CUSTARD

1¹/2 teaspoons unsalted butter

¹/4 cup chopped red bell pepper

¹/4 cup chopped green onion, white part only

¹/2 cup corn kernels (from about 1 ear)

1 tablespoon chopped fresh cilantro

1 tablespoon chopped fresh chives

4 egg yolks

1 cup heavy cream

1 teaspoon salt

¹/2 teaspoon freshly ground black pepper

Dash of Tabasco sauce

4 (1-pound) lobsters, cooked

2 tablespoons unsalted butter

¹/2 cup sliced fennel

1¹/2 cups stemmed and sliced shiitake mushrooms

1 cup cooked and sliced artichoke hearts (page 183)

¹/2 teaspoon chopped fresh cilantro

¹/2 teaspoon chopped fresh chives

¹/2 teaspoon chopped fresh thyme

SAUCE

4 tablespoons unsalted butter

¹/4 cup peeled and minced fresh ginger

1 tablespoon peeled and minced shallot

1 tablespoon tomato paste

2 teaspoons sambal (Indonesian garlic-chile paste)

2 cups heavy cream

To prepare the corn custard, preheat the oven to 350°. Generously butter 4 (1-cup) ramekins. In a small sauté pan, melt the butter over medium heat. Add the bell pepper and green onion and sauté for 2 minutes, until limp. Add the corn and cook for 2 minutes, until the vegetables are soft. Set aside to cool.

When cool, transfer to a bowl and mix in the cilantro and chives. Place 1 heaping teaspoon in each ramekin. Reserve the remaining mixture for garnish. In a bowl, whisk together the egg yolks, cream, salt, pepper, and Tabasco. Pour into the ramekins, again dividing evenly. Place the ramekins in a baking pan and pour hot water into the pan to reach halfway up the sides of the ramekins. Bake for 35 to 40 minutes, until the mixture sets.

To prepare the ragout, carefully remove the tail and claw meat from the cooked lobsters and set aside. Reserve the shells from 2 lobsters to use for making the sauce. In a sauté pan, melt the butter over medium-high heat. Add the fennel and sauté for 2 minutes, until softened. Add the mushrooms and cook for 2 minutes, until softened. Add the artichoke hearts and sauté for 2 minutes, until warmed through. Remove from the heat, stir in the cilantro, chives, and thyme and keep warm.

To prepare the sauce, chop the reserved lobster shells. In a saucepan, melt the butter over medium-high heat. Add the chopped shells, ginger, and shallot and sauté for 1 minute, until the shallot is softened. Add the tomato paste, chile paste, and cream and cook for about 15 minutes, until reduced by half. Pour through a fine-mesh sieve, discard the solids, return the liquid to the saucepan, and keep warm.

To serve, remove the custards from the ramekins by running the tip of a knife around the edges and inverting onto a plate. Slice each of the lobster tails into 4 slices. Arrange the custard, lobster claw and tail meat, and ragout in the shape of a lobster on each plate. The custard serves as the body, with the claw meat placed on either side, the ragout is spooned into the shape of the tail, and the tail meat slices laid on top of the ragout. Spoon the sauce around the plate and over the tail meat. Sprinkle the reserved corn and pepper mixture evenly over the sauce, and serve.

SERVES 4

GRILLED PORK CHOPS WITH DRIED FRUIT COMPOTE AND MOLOKA'I SWEET POTATOES

I cannot tell a lie. I created this dish for our Wailea restaurant, Joe's Bar & Grill. We get so many requests for this recipe, I thought I'd sneak it in. My idea of a pork chop, by the way, is something that's at least two inches thick and has a bone.

2 tablespoons chopped garlic
1 tablespoon olive oil
2 teaspoons chopped fresh thyme
6 (2-inch-thick) center cut pork chops
Salt
Freshly ground black pepper

DRIED FRUIT COMPOTE

1/3 cup dried cherries
1/3 cup quartered dried apricots
1/3 cup dried cranberries
4 shallots, minced
6 tablespoons sugar
1 cup port wine
2 bay leaves
1 tablespoon dried thyme

MOLOKA'I SWEET POTATOES

3 sweet potatoes, peeled and cubed
4 tablespoons unsalted butter
1 teaspoon honey
Salt
Freshly ground black pepper

To marinate the pork chops, in a small bowl, stir together the garlic, oil, and thyme. Place the chops in a shallow baking dish and season on both sides with salt and pepper. Spread the oil mixture on both sides of the chops. Cover and marinate for 4 to 6 hours in the refrigerator.

To prepare the compote, in a saucepan, combine all the ingredients over medium-low heat. Cook, stirring occasionally, for about 20 minutes, until the fruit is soft but not mushy and the liquid is reduced to a slightly thick syrup.

Prepare a fire in a charcoal grill, or preheat a gas grill.

To prepare the potatoes, bring a saucepan filled with water to a boil. Add the potatoes and boil for about 15 minutes, until tender. Drain and place in a bowl. Add the butter, honey, and salt and pepper to taste and stir to mix. Mash with a potato masher until smooth. Set aside and keep warm.

Place the chops on the grill rack and grill, turning once, for about 6 minutes on each side for meat pale pink at the center. Transfer to warmed individual plates and serve with the potatoes. Top each chop with 2 tablespoons of the compote.

SERVES 6

Grilled Quail with Sweet Corn Pudding and Maple Au Jus

Quail is my favorite poultry. It hasn't been an easy sell, so I have to put familiar tastes with it to spark people's interest. The corn pudding is to die for. This went on the menu because we were making corn pudding for lots of our catering buffets, and I wanted to create a menu item around it. For me, poultry, maple, and corn are simply fabulous together. Making your own demi-glace is quite a procedure. If you don't want to take the time to do it yourself, quality frozen brands can be found, but there's nothing like the real thing!

Demi-glace

5 pounds veal bones
1 celery stalk, coarsely chopped
1 carrot, coarsely chopped
1 onion, coarsely chopped
1 leek, white part only, coarsely chopped
2 tablespoons tomato paste
2 cups water
6 cloves garlic
1 sprig thyme
2 sprigs flat-leaf parsley
1 bay leaf
$1/2$ teaspoon black peppercorns

Marinade

$1/4$ cup freshly squeezed orange juice
2 tablespoons dry white wine
$1/2$ chipotle chile in adobo
2 cloves garlic, minced
$1/2$ teaspoon ground cumin
1 teaspoon grated orange zest

4 boneless quail

Sweet Corn Pudding

1 (14 $3/4$-ounce) can cream-style corn
1 cup corn kernels (from about 2 ears)
2 eggs

$1/4$ cup heavy cream
$1/2$ cup flour
3 tablespoons corn oil
$1/4$ teaspoon salt
$1/8$ teaspoon freshly ground black pepper
$1^1/2$ teaspoons sugar

Maple Au Jus

$1/4$ cup demi-glace (recipe above)
1 tablespoon real maple syrup

Chopped fresh cilantro, for garnish
Chopped fresh chives, for garnish

To prepare the demi-glace, preheat the oven to 450°. Place the veal bones in a single layer in a roasting pan. In a bowl, toss the celery, carrot, onion, and leek with the tomato paste and add to the pan. Roast in the oven for about 30 minutes, until the vegetables turn dark brown. Transfer the bones and vegetables to a large stockpot. Pour off the fat from the roasting pan, then deglaze the pan with the water, scraping up any browned bits on the pan bottom. Add the pan contents to the pot with the vegetables and bones over high heat. Add the garlic, thyme, parsley, bay leaf, peppercorns, and water to cover and bring to a boil. Decrease the heat to low and simmer for at least 8 hours, skimming off foam as necessary.

Strain through a sieve into a clean pot over high heat. Bring to a boil, then decrease the heat to medium and simmer for about $1^1/2$ hours, until a rich flavor is achieved. You should end up with about a quart of liquid. Freeze in small quantities for future use. To use, cook double the amount called for over medium-high heat for 20 minutes, until reduced by half.

To prepare the marinade, in a blender or food processor, combine all the ingredients and purée until smooth. Place the quail in a nonreactive dish, pour the marinade over them, and marinate for 8 hours in the refrigerator.

To prepare the pudding, preheat the oven to 375°. Lightly oil a 3-cup soufflé dish. In a food processor, combine all the ingredients and process for 10 seconds. Pour the pudding mixture into the mold. Bake for 45 minutes, until golden, puffy, and set. Do not overcook, or the custard will dry out.

Meanwhile, prepare a fire in a charcoal grill, or preheat a gas grill.

Place the quail on the grill rack and grill, turning once, for 6 to 8 minutes, until the juices run clear when a thigh is pierced. While the quail are cooking, prepare the au jus by combining the demi-glace and maple syrup in a small saucepan over low heat, and heat through.

To assemble the dish, spoon one-fourth of the corn pudding onto each plate. Lean a quail against the pudding. Ladle the au jus over quail and sprinkle with the cilantro and chives.

SERVES 4

🍃 If you think Aunt Jemima's Syrup is real maple syrup, think again. You need the real thing for this sauce to taste the way it should.

SEARED DUCK BREAST
WITH TOMATO-GINGER COMPOTE
AND WILD RICE PANCAKES

Throughout the year, the Kea Lani Hotel on Maui sponsors food events called Grand Chefs on Tour. Island chefs are paired with "celebrity" mainland chefs to share the spotlight for a weekend of cooking classes and food and wine dinners. They are too much fun! This is a dish I created for one of those dinners.

MARINADE

$1/2$ cup pineapple juice

$1/4$ cup peanut oil

1 tablespoon honey

1 tablespoon plus $1^1/2$ teaspoons soy sauce

1 tablespoon peeled and finely chopped
    fresh ginger

2 tablespoons Dijon mustard

$1^1/2$ teaspoons Asian sesame oil

$1^1/2$ teaspoons chopped fresh mint

$1^1/2$ teaspoons five-spice powder

2 (12-ounce) boneless whole duck breasts

TOMATO-GINGER COMPOTE

2 cups seeded and coarsely chopped tomato

$1/2$ cup coarsely chopped onion

$1/4$ cup peeled and coarsely chopped
    fresh ginger

3 whole star anise

1 teaspoon five-spice powder

$1^1/2$ teaspoons Asian sesame oil

1 tablespoon plum sauce

$1/2$ teaspoon salt

Freshly ground black pepper

Chicken stock, for thinning (see page 10)

WILD RICE PANCAKES

$1^1/2$ tablespoons unsalted butter

$1/3$ cup peeled and finely chopped carrot

$1/3$ cup finely chopped celery

$1/2$ cup finely chopped yellow onion

Pinch of dried thyme

1 egg

$1/3$ cup milk

1 cup cooked wild rice

$1/4$ cup finely chopped green onion, green part only

$1/3$ cup toasted slivered almonds

$1/4$ cup flour

$1/2$ teaspoon salt

Freshly ground black pepper

Vegetable oil, for brushing griddle

To prepare the marinade, in a bowl, combine all the ingredients and whisk until well mixed.

Cut the duck breasts in half, prick all over with a fork, score through the skin with 3 cuts, and place in a shallow nonreactive dish. Pour the marinade over the breasts, cover, and marinate overnight in the refrigerator.

Preheat the oven to 350°. To prepare the compote, in a baking dish, combine the tomato, onion, ginger, star anise, five-spice powder, and sesame oil. Roast for 20 minutes, until tender. Remove and discard the star anise. Transfer the compote to the bowl of a food processor fitted with a metal blade. Pulse several times until the mixture is coarsely puréed. Add the plum sauce and season with salt and pepper. Thin to desired consistency with a little chicken stock and keep warm.

To prepare the pancakes, in a heavy skillet, melt the butter over medium heat. Add the carrot, celery, onion, and thyme and sauté for 8 to 10 minutes, until the carrot is tender, being careful not to brown the vegetables. Transfer the mixture to a bowl. In a small bowl, whisk together the egg and milk until blended. Add the wild rice, green onion, and almonds to the carrot mixture and stir in the egg mixture. Stir in the flour, salt, and pepper to taste.

Heat a griddle over medium-high heat and brush it with vegetable oil. Using a heaping 1/4-cup measure, scoop the batter onto the griddle. Cook, turning once, for 2 to 3 minutes on each side, until golden. Transfer to a plate and keep warm.

Preheat the oven to 375°. Remove the duck from the marinade and pat dry.

Place a nonstick ovenproof sauté pan over high heat. When the pan is hot, add the breasts and sear on both sides until browned. Cover the pan with aluminum foil. Bake for 12 to 15 minutes for medium rare or until done to taste. Remove from the oven and thinly slice on the diagonal.

To serve, fan out 5 to 6 slices of duck on each warmed individual plate and top with the compote. Serve the wild rice pancakes alongside.

SERVES 4

Tandoori Chicken with Fruit and Nut Basmati Rice

I am a big fan of Indian cooking, but unfortunately it is a cuisine that has largely eluded the Islands. Every so often I like to put an item on the menu that fulfills my need to taste the exotic flavors of that part of the world. And judging by how much of this dish we sell, our guests enjoy those flavors too.

2 tablespoons freshly squeezed lime juice

3 tablespoons peeled and diced fresh ginger

6 cloves garlic

2 teaspoons paprika

1 teaspoon ground cardamom

2 teaspoons ground cumin

2 teaspoons crushed red pepper flakes

1 tablespoon garam masala (Indian spice mix)

1/4 cup olive oil

1 cup plain yogurt

6 boneless, skinless chicken breast halves

6 sprigs mint, for garnish

Fruit and Nut Basmati Rice

3 cups basmati rice

4 tablespoons olive oil

1/2 cup chopped onion

2 teaspoons peeled and minced fresh ginger

5 cloves garlic, minced

1/8 teaspoon ground cloves

1/8 teaspoon ground cardamom

1/2 teaspoon ground cinnamon

1 teaspoon ground turmeric

1 cup frozen coconut milk, thawed

2 cups water

2 teaspoons salt

1/4 cup raisins

1/4 cup diced dried cherries

1/4 diced dried apricots

1/4 cup pine nuts, toasted (page 106)

To prepare the marinade, in a blender or food processor, combine the lime juice, ginger, garlic, paprika, cardamom, cumin, pepper flakes, and garam masala and process to mix. Add the olive oil and yogurt and blend until smooth.

Place the chicken breasts in a shallow dish and pour the marinade over them. Turn the chicken to coat well, cover, and refrigerate overnight.

Preheat the oven to 375°. Spray a baking dish with vegetable-oil cooking spray.

Remove the chicken from the marinade and shake off the excess liquid. Place the marinade into a saucepan and bring to a rolling boil over medium heat for 2 minutes. Set aside about 1/2 cup of the marinade for serving. Arrange the chicken in the prepared baking dish and bake, basting frequently with the remaining marinade, for 35 to 40 minutes, until the juices run clear when the meat is pierced.

To prepare the rice, place the rice in a colander and rinse under cold running water for 2 minutes. Set aside to drain.

In a saucepan, heat the olive oil over medium heat. Add the onion, ginger, and garlic and sauté for 2 minutes, until the onion starts to wilt. Add the cloves, cardamom, cinnamon, and turmeric and sauté for 3 minutes longer. Add the rice and sauté for 5 minutes, until the rice begins to cook. Add the coconut milk, water, and salt, increase the heat to medium-high, and bring to a boil. Decrease the heat to low, cover, and cook for 10 minutes. Add the raisins, cherries, and apricots and continue to cook, covered, for 10 minutes, until the rice is tender and the liquid has been absorbed. Remove from the heat and keep covered until ready to use. Just before serving, stir in the pine nuts.

To serve, place one-sixth of the rice in the middle of a plate. Top with a chicken breast and spoon on a small amount of the reserved marinade. Garnish each serving with a sprig of mint.

SERVES 6

SZECHUAN BARBECUED SALMON
HGS CLASSIC

When we opened the restaurant, we started out serving good food without much thought to influences. But as Hawai'i Regional Cuisine got going, more and more Asian-influenced dishes showed up on the menu. This was one of those dishes Chef Tom developed during a time when salmon, for some reason, just wasn't plentiful on the islands, so we could only serve this as a special when we were able to get really fresh salmon. Now, after almost a decade, it is a Hali'imaile General Store classic and fresh salmon is consistently available. We even have one customer who doesn't really care for salmon, but who orders it almost every time she dines with us.

SZECHUAN SAUCE

1¹/2 teaspoons olive oil

1/2 onion, chopped

3 cloves garlic

1¹/2-inch piece fresh ginger, peeled and chopped

1/2 lemongrass stalk, white part only, chopped

3 fresh basil leaves, chopped

2 tablespoons brown sugar

1 tablespoon plus 1¹/2 teaspoons rice vinegar

1/2 jalapeño chile, seeded

1 teaspoon toasted and ground Szechuan
  peppercorns (see note)

HOT-AND-SOUR SAUCE

1/2 cup vegetable stock

2 teaspoons honey

2 teaspoons rice vinegar

1 teaspoon red wine vinegar

1 teaspoon soy sauce

1/4 teaspoon chopped garlic

1/4 teaspoon sambal (Indonesian garlic-chile paste)

4 cups mixed salad greens, including spinach,
  frisée, won bok (Chinese cabbage), and
  baby bok choy

4 (6-ounce) salmon fillets

To prepare the Szechuan sauce, in a skillet, heat the oil over medium heat. Add the onion and garlic and sauté, stirring, for 5 minutes, until caramelized. Allow to cool.

Meanwhile, prepare a fire in a charcoal grill, or preheat a gas grill.

To finish the sauce, in a food processor, combine the onion-garlic mixture, ginger, lemongrass, basil, sugar, vinegar, jalapeño, and peppercorns and purée until well blended.

To make the hot-and-sour sauce, in a bowl, mix together all the ingredients.

In a bowl, toss the greens with the hot-and-sour sauce. Place the dressed greens in a large sauté pan over medium-high heat, and cook for about 2 minutes, until limp. Keep warm.

Preheat the broiler. Place the salmon on the grill rack and grill, turning once, for 5 minutes on each side for rare. Transfer to a broiler pan. Spread the Szechuan sauce evenly over 1 side of each fillet. Slip under the broiler for 2 minutes to caramelize the topping.

Divide the greens among individual plates and top each with a salmon fillet. Serve at once.

SERVES 4

Szechuan peppercorns are not true peppercorns. They are seeds from a tree native to the Chinese province of Szechuan. To toast them, heat a dry sauté pan over high heat. Add the peppercorns and cook for about 1¹/2 minutes, until they release a fragrance. Remove from the heat and grind in a spice grinder or electric coffee grinder.

Herb-Roasted Filet Mignon with Grilled Jumbo Prawns and Mushroom Ragout

There's nothing like a great filet mignon. The sauce that goes over it should be one that enhances the flavor of the meat. A good mushroom sauce is all this exquisite cut needs.

1 tablespoon minced garlic

2 tablespoons chopped mixed fresh herbs such as basil, cilantro, thyme, rosemary, chervil, and tarragon

2 tablespoons extra virgin olive oil

6 (6-ounce) filet mignons

12 jumbo prawns, peeled with tail segment intact, and deveined

1 tablespoon dry sherry

2 teaspoons peeled and minced fresh ginger

1 teaspoon grated lemon zest

2 tablespoons olive oil

MUSHROOM RAGOUT

1 cup dried morel mushrooms

6 1/2 tablespoons unsalted butter, at room temperature

1/2 cup sliced shiitake mushrooms

3/4 cup medium-dry Madeira

1 cup demi-glace (page 112)

1 1/2 teaspoons flour

2 tablespoons chopped fresh flat-leaf parsley

Rosemary sprigs, for garnish

🌿 Searing beef fillets over high heat ensures the juices will stay in as the meat cooks.

To marinate the beef, in a small bowl, mix together the garlic, herbs, and olive oil. Place the filets in a shallow dish, rub with the oil mixture, cover, and marinate for 4 to 5 hours in the refrigerator.

To marinate the prawns, lay them in a shallow dish. In a small bowl, mix together the sherry, ginger, lemon zest, and olive oil and pour over the prawns. Marinate for 1 hour at room temperature.

To prepare the ragout, soak the morels in warm water to cover for 15 minutes, until softened. Rinse and soak again for 10 minutes. Repeat the process 3 or 4 times, until no dirt remains. Drain well.

Preheat the oven to 375°.

In a heavy sauté pan, melt 4 tablespoons of the butter over medium-high heat. Add the shiitake mushrooms and sauté for 2 minutes, until just cooked. Add the morels and sauté for 3 minutes, until the mushrooms begin to brown. Add the Madeira and cook for 2 minutes, until the liquid is nearly evaporated. Decrease the heat to low, add the demi-glace, and cook for 6 minutes, until reduced by one-third. Combine the 1 1/2 teaspoons butter with the flour to form a paste (called a beurre manié). Swirl into the mushrooms and simmer for 1 minute to thicken. Keep warm until serving. Just before serving, swirl in the remaining 2 tablespoons butter and stir in the parsley.

To cook the beef, heat a large ovenproof sauté pan over high heat until hot. Add the filets and sear for 30 seconds to 1 minute per side, until caramelized. Place in the oven for 5 to 7 minutes for medium rare or to desired doneness.

Meanwhile, to cook the prawns, place a clean sauté pan over medium-high heat. Remove the prawns from the marinade and place in the pan. Cook for about 2 minutes, until they just begin to curl and turn pink.

Place a filet on each warm plate. Top with 2 prawns. Ladle the sauce around the filet. Garnish the shrimp with the rosemary sprigs. Serve at once.

SERVES 6

Smoked Chicken and Wild Mushroom Pasta

On the very first menu at Hali'imaile General Store, we had a smoked chicken bought from a supplier, which we served with pineapple chutney. As we progressed into the life of a restaurant, I couldn't bring myself to keep something on the menu that hadn't been cooked on site. I created this dish to satisfy the people who came in saying, "Where's the smoked chicken?" We use oyster sauce to give it a bit of Asian flair. It was on the menu for a couple of years, and when we opened Joe's, we put it on that menu, where it periodically reappears.

2 1/2 tablespoons unsalted butter

3 shallots, minced

1 green onion, white part only, sliced

1 cup stemmed and sliced button mushrooms

2 cups stemmed and sliced shiitake mushrooms

1 1/2 teaspoons flour

3 cups chicken stock, heated (see page 10)

2 tablespoons dry sherry

1 1/2 teaspoons oyster sauce

1 1/2 teaspoons freshly squeezed lemon juice

1 cup heavy cream

1/2 pound dried orrechiette pasta

12 ounces smoked chicken meat, shredded

Chopped green onion, green part only, for garnish

Grated Parmesan cheese, for garnish

Toasted pine nuts (see page 106), for garnish

In a large saucepan, melt 2 tablespoons of the butter over medium-high heat. Add the shallots and green onion and sauté for 2 minutes, until limp. Add the button mushrooms and 1 cup of the shiitake mushrooms and sauté for 4 minutes, until all the moisture is absorbed. Sprinkle the flour over the mushrooms and stir to mix. Pour in the chicken stock, while stirring continuously. Add the sherry, oyster sauce, and lemon juice and boil, stirring occasionally, for 15 minutes, until the mixture thickens and the mushrooms are cooked. Decrease the heat to medium-low, add the cream, and simmer for another 10 minutes, until reduced by one-half. Strain through a sieve, capturing the liquid and discarding the solids. The sauce should be thick enough to coat a spoon. Return to the saucepan if it is not thick enough and reduce over medium-high heat.

In a sauté pan, melt the remaining 1/2 tablespoon butter over medium heat. Add the remaining 1 cup shiitake mushrooms and sauté for 2 minutes, until softened. Add this mixture to the sauce and heat through.

Meanwhile, bring a large pot of salted water to a boil. Add the pasta, stir well, and cook for about 10 minutes, until al dente.

Drain the pasta and place in a serving dish. Add the sauce and chicken and toss to coat evenly. Garnish with green onion, Parmesan, and pine nuts and serve.

SERVES 4

RACK OF LAMB WITH MINT PESTO AND WARM GORGONZOLA POTATO SALAD

Okay, okay, I know all the store regulars are looking for our Hunan lamb recipe, the one we can't change or our customers will start a riot. Well, you'll just have to keep coming to the restaurant to eat it. This recipe is our first runner-up in the lamb category. I think you'll enjoy it, too.

MINT PESTO

2 cups packed fresh mint leaves

3 cloves garlic, minced

1/2 cup pepitas (toasted pumpkin seeds)

1 tablespoon good-quality red wine vinegar

1/4 cup extra virgin olive oil

1/2 teaspoon salt

1/2 teaspoon freshly ground black pepper

WARM GORGONZOLA POTATO SALAD

20 small new potatoes (about 2 pounds)

2 tablespoons olive oil

1 cup sliced shiitake mushrooms

1 red onion, thinly sliced

1/4 cup chopped fresh chives

1/2 cup crumbled Gorgonzola cheese

2 (8-bone) lamb racks

To prepare the pesto, in a food processor, combine the mint leaves, garlic, and *pepitas* and pulse several times. With the motor running, add the vinegar and drizzle in the oil through the feed tube and process until well combined. Transfer to a bowl and add the salt and pepper.

To prepare the salad, in a saucepan combine the potatoes with water to cover and bring to a boil. Cook for about 10 minutes, until tender. Drain, quarter the potatoes, and keep warm in a large bowl. Preheat the oven to 400°.

In a sauté pan, heat the olive oil over medium-high heat. Add the mushrooms and sauté for about 3 minutes, until just cooked. If the pan dries out, add 1 tablespoon of water so the mushrooms won't scorch. Add to the potatoes along with the onion and chives and toss together. Add the Gorgonzola and toss again. Keep warm.

Heat a large nonstick ovenproof sauté pan over high heat until hot. No oil is needed. Using tongs, sear the lamb racks for 30 seconds to 1 minute on the loin side, until caramelized. Remove the racks from the sauté pan and spread one-half of the pesto over the top of each rack. Return the racks to the pan, place in the oven, and roast for 10 to 12 minutes for medium rare or to desired doneness.

Cut each rack into 4 double chops and transfer 2 to each warmed individual plate. Serve with the warm potato salad.

SERVES 4

If you make extra pesto, it can be stored in an airtight container in the refrigerator for up to 2 weeks. There are many uses for pesto, including hot and cold pasta dishes, as well as placing it under the skin of chicken breasts before grilling.

ONE GOOD THING ON TOP OF ANOTHER

What are the good things? They are layers of unagi (freshwater eel), crab, and avocado between baked lumpia wrappers. I created this dish for a Big Island Bounty luncheon that I did with chefs Amy Ferguson-Ota and Elka Gilmore. The name says it all.

GINGER OIL

1/4 cup ground ginger

3 tablespoons water

1 cup grapeseed or safflower oil

SUSHI RICE

1 cup short-grain white rice

2 cups plus 2 tablespoons water

1/4 cup rice vinegar

1 1/2 teaspoons sugar

1 teaspoon salt

4 lumpia wrappers

3 tablespoons Asian sesame oil

6 ounces smoked unagi (freshwater eel), thinly sliced on the diagonal

1 cup cooked Dungeness crabmeat

1/2 cup peeled, seeded, and finely chopped tomato

2 teaspoons chopped fresh mint

2 tablespoons good-quality mayonnaise

2 teaspoons wasabi paste

1 teaspoon peeled and finely chopped fresh ginger

1 tablespoon furikake (Japanese spice mix)

1/2 cup peeled, seeded, and finely diced cucumber

16 thin avocado slices

1 ounce daikon sprouts

1 teaspoon tobiko (flying fish roe)

2 teaspoons green tobiko (flying fish roe flavored with wasabi)

To prepare the ginger oil, in a bowl, whisk the ginger with the water to form a paste. Gradually whisk in the oil. Pour into a jar, cover, and let stand at room temperature for at least 2 days or up to 1 week. Carefully pour the clear oil into a jar and discard the ginger sediment left behind. (The oil can be kept covered in the refrigerator indefinitely.)

To prepare the sushi rice, place the rice in a sieve and rinse under cold running water until the water runs clear. Place in a saucepan, add the water, and bring to a boil over high heat. Cover, reduce the heat to low, and cook for 12 to 14 minutes, until the rice is tender and all the liquid is absorbed.

Meanwhile, in a small saucepan, combine the vinegar, sugar, and salt over medium heat. Stir until the sugar dissolves, then bring the mixture to a boil. Remove from the heat and allow to cool.

Transfer the rice to a wooden bowl. With a rice paddle or broad wooden spoon, slowly stir the vinegar mixture into the hot rice, continuously moving and turning the rice. Cover the bowl with a towel to keep warm.

To prepare the lumpia wrappers, preheat the oven to 400°. Brush 2 wrappers generously with the sesame oil. Top each with another wrapper. Brush with more sesame oil. Cut each into 4 triangles. Place the triangles on a baking sheet and bake for 6 to 8 minutes, until golden brown. Remove from the oven, decrease the oven temperature to 350°, and allow to cool.

Spray a baking sheet with vegetable-oil cooking spray. Place the eel slices on the prepared sheet and bake for 8 minutes, until heated through. Remove from the oven and keep warm.

In a bowl, combine the crabmeat, tomato, mint, mayonnaise, wasabi paste, and ginger and stir to bind. Mix the warm sushi rice with the *furikake* and cucumber. Keep warm.

Form the rice into 4 straight-sided cakes, each about 1 inch tall and 2 inches in diameter and place on individual plates. Top each cake with a lumpia triangle. Fan 4 avocado slices atop each triangle. Divide the crab mixture evenly among the cakes. Top

with the daikon sprouts, again dividing evenly. Place another lumpia triangle on top. Divide the eel evenly and place on the triangles. Drizzle each serving with 1 teaspoon of the ginger oil. Sprinkle the two kinds of tobiko all over the 4 plates. Drizzle the plates with the remaining ginger oil and serve immediately.

SERVES 4

🌺 *Furikake* is a dry Japanese rice seasoning. A variety of different combinations of the main ingredients—sesame seeds, seaweed, shaved bonita (a Japanese fish that has been dried), soy sauce, sugar, and salt—can be found.

ITALASIA SHRIMP AND SCALLOP PASTA

A well-made basil pesto sauce is a staple of any Italian kitchen. My love for cilantro led me to a cilantro-based pesto that became a hit with our customers along with the unique name that Bonnie created.

CILANTRO PESTO

1/4 cup whole macadamia nuts, toasted (page 106)

2 cloves garlic

1 1/2 cups chopped fresh cilantro

1/3 cup grated Parmesan cheese

1 teaspoon salt

1/2 teaspoon freshly ground black pepper

1/2 cup olive oil

1/2 pound dried farfalle pasta

2 cups heavy cream

2 tablespoons unsalted butter

1 pound peeled and deveined shrimp

1 pound sea scallops

2 tablespoons grated Parmesan cheese

To prepare the pesto, in a food processor, combine the nuts, garlic, and cilantro and pulse until a paste forms. Add the Parmesan cheese, salt, and pepper and pulse a few times. With the motor running, add the oil through the feed tube and process until the pesto is thick and smooth. Measure out 1/2 cup of the pesto and set aside for this dish. Put the remaining pesto in an airtight container and store in the refrigerator for up to 2 weeks, or in the freezer for up to 3 months.

Bring a large pot filled with salted water to a boil. Add the pasta, stir well, and cook for 6 to 8 minutes, until al dente. Be careful not to overcook. Drain, place in a warmed bowl, and toss with 2 tablespoons of the pesto. Cover to keep warm.

Place the cream and the remaining 6 tablespoons pesto in a saucepan and bring to a boil over medium-high heat. Reduce the heat to medium-low and simmer for about 10 minutes, until the sauce reduces and thickens. While the sauce is reducing, melt the butter in a sauté pan over medium-high heat. Add the shrimp and scallops and sauté for 3 to 4 minutes, until almost cooked. Pour the reduced sauce over the shrimp and scallops and heat for a few minutes longer, until the seafood is cooked through.

Pour the sauce over the pasta and toss to coat. Sprinkle with the Parmesan cheese and serve.

SERVES 4

Banana-Caramel Custard Cake

One day, my dad brought in a big stalk of bananas from a tree in his yard. It was huge, actually, and I thought, "What will I do with all these?" I decided to make a banana cake and then put extra bananas in the cake. Then I thought I'd put caramel in the cake. Yum! Then I just got carried away. . . . — T.G.

Banana Cake

2 cups cake flour

1 teaspoon baking soda

1 teaspoon baking powder

$^1/_2$ teaspoon salt

$^1/_2$ cup plus 2 tablespoons unsalted butter,
    at room temperature

1 cup sugar

2 eggs

$1^1/_2$ teaspoons vanilla extract

3 ripe bananas

$^1/_2$ cup sour cream

1 cup caramel filling (page 188)

4 cups buttercream frosting (page 40)

4 bananas, sliced

1 cup pastry cream (page 184)

To prepare the cake, preheat the oven to 350°. Butter and flour an 8 by 3-inch round cake pan.

In a bowl, sift together the flour, baking soda, baking powder, and salt. In another bowl, using an electric mixer on medium speed, cream together the butter and sugar until fluffy. Add the eggs and vanilla and beat well.

In a bowl, mash the bananas with a fork. Add the sour cream and mix well. Add the flour mixture in $1^1/_2$ cup batches to the butter mixture, alternating with the banana mixture, beginning with the flour mixture and ending with the banana mixture.

Pour the batter into the prepared pan. Bake for 40 minutes, until a toothpick inserted into the center comes out clean. Remove from the oven, turn out of the pan onto a rack, and allow to cool. You can refrigerate the cake for a couple of hours to make it easier to manipulate.

Using a serrated knife, cut the cake horizontally into 3 layers. Place 1 layer on a serving plate. Add 3 tablespoons of the caramel filling to the buttercream. On the first layer of cake, fan out enough banana slices to cover the cake. Cover with half of the remaining caramel filling and then with half of the pastry cream. Place another cake layer on top and cover with the remaining banana slices, caramel filling, and pastry cream. Place the third layer on top and cover the whole cake with the buttercream. Cover and refrigerate for 2 to 3 hours. Serve chilled.

SERVES 8

I use Tahitian vanilla, which is the best, but any pure vanilla extract will do.

MACADAMIA NUT–MACAROON PRALINE CAKE

For this cake, I adapted an old French recipe I learned while working at Le Nôtre in Plasir, France. It was originally almond meringue, and I switched all the flavors so that the cake would work with macadamia nuts. It's sort of a sophisticated French-Hawaiian dessert. — T.G.

MERINGUE RING

1¼ cups macadamia nut pieces, toasted and
    chopped (page 106)

1¼ cups confectioners' sugar

2 tablespoons flour

3 tablespoons milk

8 egg whites

Pinch of salt

½ cup granulated sugar

1 recipe baked white butter cake (page 43)

½ cup simple syrup (page 44)

1 tablespoon dark rum, preferably Myers's

MACADAMIA NUT PRALINE

2 cups chopped macadamia nuts

1½ cups granulated sugar

1 tablespoon water

3 cups buttercream frosting (page 40)

1½ cups dark chocolate mousse (page 184)

Confectioners' sugar, for dusting

1 cup crème anglaise (page 188)

Before you begin making the meringue, line 2 baking sheets with parchment paper and draw an 8-inch circle in the center of each. Turn the paper over. This will be your guide whether you decide to pipe the meringues or spread them onto the circles with a spatula.

To make the meringue ring, preheat the oven to 250°. In a food processor, combine the nuts, confectioners' sugar, and flour and pulse to the consistency of a coarse meal. Place in a bowl and add the milk. Stir to form a paste.

In a bowl, using an electric mixer on medium speed, whip the egg whites and salt until soft peaks form. Increase the speed to high, add the granulated sugar, and beat until the mixture forms medium peaks.

Fold half of the egg whites into the nut mixture, then fold in the remaining whites. Do not overmix. Spoon the meringue into a pastry bag fitted with a plain ½-inch tip and pipe onto the circles on the parchment paper. Alternatively, spread the meringue on the circles with a spatula.

Bake for 3 hours, until golden brown. Remove from the oven and allow to cool. Increase the oven temperature to 350°.

Using a serrated knife, cut the butter cake into 2 layers. Reserve 1 layer in the freezer for future use. Place the remaining layer on a plate. Combine the simple syrup and rum and soak the cake.

To prepare the praline, line a baking sheet with parchment paper. In a bowl, toss the nuts with the sugar and water. Turn out onto the prepared baking sheet and spread evenly. Bake for 10 to 15 minutes, until the nuts darken and the sugar starts to caramelize. Allow to cool completely.

Transfer the cooled praline to a food processor and process until it resembles a coarse meal. In a bowl, add half of the praline to the buttercream and stir to mix.

Assemble the cake on a plate in this order: meringue, mousse, butter cake, 1¹/₂ cups of the praline buttercream, and meringue. Cover the sides with the remaining buttercream and pat the remaining praline onto the buttercream. Dust with confectioners' sugar, cover, and refrigerate for 2 hours. Serve with a pool of crème anglaise under each piece of cake.

SERVES 8

PINEAPPLE PIE

I was making apple pie in 1989, when movie mogul George Grief, a friend of my dad's, walked in and asked, "Why don't you make pineapple pie?" It had never occurred to me. I took my apple pie recipe, the same spices—cinnamon, ginger, nutmeg, cloves—and the same crust, and replaced the apples with pineapple. I put it in the oven and while it was baking, I knew this was the ticket. It's Bonnie's personal favorite, in spite of the fact that she's a chocoholic. So that's saying a lot about this pie. It's a great holiday alternative to apple pie. But should you want to make it apple instead, you can easily substitute any baking apples for the pineapple. The quantities are all the same. The apple version, by the way, brings tears of joy to both my brother-in-law Greg and my dad.—T.G.

2 recipes sweet dough (page 78)

PINEAPPLE FILLING

5 cups chopped pineapple (2 large pineapples)
1¹/2 cups firmly packed dark brown sugar
³/4 cup cornstarch
2 teaspoons ground cinnamon
2 teaspoons ground ginger
2 tablespoons unsalted butter, cut into small pieces

2 tablespoons sugar
¹/2 teaspoon ground nutmeg

Spray an 8-inch fluted tart pan with a removable bottom with vegetable-oil cooking spray. After chilling the sweet dough, divide it in half. On a floured surface, roll out the first half to ¹/4 inch thick and 10 inches in diameter and carefully transfer to the prepared pan. Press into the bottom and sides of the pan. Using a rolling pin, press down on the pan edges to remove the excess dough. Roll out the remaining half of the dough to ¹/4 inch thick and 9 inches in diameter. Without covering, refrigerate the lined pan and the round for at least 20 minutes, or up to 2 hours.

Preheat the oven to 325°.

To prepare the filling, in a bowl, mix together all the ingredients except the butter. Pour into the unbaked pie shell. Scatter the butter pieces on top. Carefully lay the dough round on top of the filling, it's not necessary to seal the edges. In a small bowl, mix together the sugar and nutmeg until well blended. Brush the pie with water and sprinkle with the nutmeg sugar.

Bake for 1¹/2 hours, until the pineapple starts to bubble along the edges. Transfer to a rack and allow to cool until warm. To unmold, remove the pan sides and slide the pie onto a serving plate. Serve warm or at room temperature.

SERVES 6 TO 8

PUMPKIN-PECAN CHEESECAKE

I make this fall-flavored cheesecake because it is perfect at Thanksgiving time. If I don't take it off the menu before December 1, Beverly says, "Lose the pumpkin cheesecake." I like to garnish this cheese-cake with sweetened whipped cream spiced with nutmeg. — T.G.

CRUST

2 cups graham cracker crumbs

1/4 cup sugar

1/4 cup pecans, chopped

1/2 teaspoon ground ginger

7 tablespoons unsalted butter, melted

CHEESECAKE MIX

1 1/2 pounds cream cheese, at room temperature

2 cups sugar

1/2 cup sour cream

1 cup pumpkin purée

1/2 teaspoon ground cinnamon

1/2 teaspoon ground ginger

1/4 teaspoon ground cloves

3 eggs

To prepare the crust, in a bowl, mix together the crumbs, sugar, nuts, and ginger. Pour in the butter and toss to combine. Spray a 10-inch fluted tart pan with a removable bottom with vegetable-oil cooking spray. Press the mixture into the bottom and sides of the prepared pan.

Preheat the oven to 300°. To prepare the cheesecake mix, in a bowl, using an electric mixer on medium speed, cream together the cream cheese, sugar, and sour cream until fluffy. Add the pumpkin purée, cinnamon, ginger, and cloves and beat until well incorporated. Scrape down the sides of the bowl and add the eggs, one at a time, beating well after each addition.

Pour the cheesecake mix into the crust. Bake for 1 hour. Turn off the oven and let the cheesecake sit in the oven for 1 1/2 hours longer. Allow to cool. Cover and refrigerate for 4 to 6 hours. To unmold, remove the pan sides and slide the cake onto a serving plate.

SERVES 8

Liliko'i Meringue Pie with Gingerbread Crust

The French do lemon meringue, and I decided to do liliko'i because it's a great local flavor . . . and because we're here. I love liliko'i and so do most residents and visitors. The tangy flavor works really well with the gingerbread. — T.G.

Gingerbread Crust

6 tablespoons unsalted butter, at room temperature

1/3 cup firmly packed dark brown sugar

1/4 cup dark molasses

1 egg

1 1/2 cups flour

1/2 teaspoon baking soda

1/2 teaspoon ground ginger

1/4 teaspoon ground nutmeg

1/2 teaspoon ground cinnamon

1/4 teaspoon ground cloves

1/4 teaspoon salt

Liliko'i Curd

6 whole eggs

6 egg yolks

1 1/3 cups sugar

1 1/4 cups liliko'i purée (page 38) or passion fruit purée (page 15)

Meringue

6 egg whites

1 cup sugar

To prepare the crust, in a bowl, using an electric mixer on medium speed, cream together the butter, sugar, and molasses. Add the egg and mix well. In another bowl, sift together the flour, baking soda, ginger, nutmeg, cinnamon, cloves, and salt.

Add the flour mixture to the creamed mixture and beat just until all ingredients are incorporated. Do not overwork the dough. Press into a square on a piece of plastic wrap, enclose in the plastic, and refrigerate for 1 hour.

Preheat the oven to 350°. Spray an 8-inch fluted tart pan with a removable bottom with vegetable-oil cooking spray. On a floured surface, roll out the dough to 1/4 inch thick and 10 inches in diameter and carefully transfer to the prepared pan. Press into the bottom and sides of the pan. Using a rolling pin, press down on the pan edges to trim off the excess dough. This dough is very soft so you must work quickly. Refrigerate for 20 minutes.

Bake the crust for 20 minutes, until light golden brown. Remove from the oven and allow to cool.

To prepare the curd, in a stainless-steel or other heatproof bowl that will fit over the top of a pan of boiling water, whisk together the whole eggs and egg yolks until blended. Add the sugar and liliko'i purée and mix well. Place the bowl on top of a pan of boiling water and whisk continuously for 10 to 15 minutes, until the mixture thickens and has the consistency of a thick pudding. Immediately pour into the baked crust. Cover and refrigerate for 2 hours.

To prepare the meringue, in a bowl, combine the egg whites and sugar. Place over a pan of simmering water and whisk continuously until warm. Remove from the heat and whip until cool.

Spoon the meringue into a pastry bag fitted with a 1/2-inch star tip and pipe rosettes on top of the pie. Use a butane torch to lightly color the top, or slip briefly under a preheated broiler. Return the tart to the refrigerator and chill for 1 hour, until completely set. To unmold, remove the pan sides and slide the pie onto a serving plate. Serve chilled.

SERVES 6

MINI PARTY SWEETS

I MAKE THESE THREE RECIPES AND SERVE THEM TOGETHER FOR LOTS
OF PARTIES. WHEN PEOPLE SAY THEY WANT PETITS FOURS,
THIS IS WHAT I THINK THEY MEAN. —T.G.

MYERS'S RUM CHOCOLATE TRUFFLES

This is a French recipe, to which I've added extra rum. Everyone loves them.—T.G.

3/4 cup heavy cream
1/4 cup dark rum, preferably Myers's
8 ounces semisweet chocolate

DIPPING CHOCOLATE
8 ounces semisweet chocolate
1/4 cup cocoa powder

To prepare the truffle balls, in a saucepan, combine the cream and rum and bring to a boil over medium heat. Remove from the heat and stir in the chocolate until melted. Let cool. Cover and refrigerate overnight.

The next day, have ready a cup or so of very hot tap water and a melon baller. To form the truffle balls, dip the melon baller into the hot water, shake off the excess water, and then scoop up the chocolate mix, placing the balls on a sheet pan lined with waxed paper. Refrigerate the truffles for about 1^1/2 hours.

To prepare the dipping chocolate, place the chocolate in a small heatproof bowl and rest in the top of a saucepan of barely simmering water. Heat until melted, then stir until smooth. Remove from the heat and allow to cool. Line a baking sheet with waxed paper and spread the cocoa on it. One by one, drop the truffles into the melted chocolate and, using a fork, place them on the cocoa. Refrigerate for 20 minutes and then roll in the cocoa. Dust off the excess cocoa. Store in a covered container in the refrigerator, but bring back to room temperature before serving.

MAKES ABOUT 30 TRUFFLES

PINEAPPLE SHORTBREAD COOKIES

We're in the middle of a pineapple field! In addition to parties, I use these cookies to decorate the Piña Colada Cheesecake (page 37). They're great Christmas tree decorations, too. — T.G.

1 recipe sweet dough (page 78)
Raw sugar, for sprinkling
Ground nutmeg, for sprinkling
3 tablespoons apricot-pineapple preserves

Preheat the oven to 350°.

On a floured surface, roll out the dough to ¼ inch thick. Using a pineapple-shaped cookie cutter, or any other cookie cutter shape, cut out as many cookies as possible (gather and reroll the scraps once to cut out additional cookies). These are sandwich cookies, so you'll need 2 pineapples for each completed cookie.

Divide the cutouts evenly between 2 ungreased baking sheets. On the sheet of cutouts for the cookie tops, score the dough in a crisscross pattern, using the back of a small paring knife. Brush with water and sprinkle with the raw sugar and nutmeg.

Place both baking sheets in the oven on 2 separate racks and bake for 10 minutes. Switch the trays between the racks, rotate them, and bake for another 10 minutes, until all the cookies are a light golden brown. Allow to cool completely on the baking sheets.

Spread the preserves on the bottom cookies and close with the tops. Store in an airtight container at room temperature.

MAKES ABOUT 18 COOKIES

LILIKO'I BARS

I modified a lemon bar recipe without at first realizing that liliko'i purée has a lot more sugar than lemon purée does. The bars came out completely flat for a while. I had to play with this recipe for a long time. — T.G.

1 recipe sweet dough (page 84)

LILIKO'I FILLING

6 eggs

2 cups granulated sugar

1/4 cup plus 2 tablespoons flour

1 1/2 teaspoons baking powder

2/3 cup liliko'i purée (page 38) or passion fruit purée (page 15)

Confectioners' sugar, for dusting

Carefully press the dough into the bottom and halfway up the sides of a 9 by 13-inch pan to 1/2 inch thick. (Make sure the crust is pressed halfway up the sides of the pan, or the filling will leak underneath.) Refrigerate for 20 minutes. Meanwhile, preheat the oven to 300°.

Bake for 15 minutes, until the edges start to brown. Set aside and allow to cool completely.

To prepare the filling, in a bowl, whisk the eggs until blended. One by one, whisk in the granulated sugar, then the flour, then the baking powder, and finally the purée, to ensure a smooth filling. Pour into the prebaked crust. Bake for an additional 35 to 40 minutes, until the top is golden brown. Allow to cool completely, then cover and refrigerate for 2 to 3 hours.

Cut into 1 by 1-inch squares and dust with confectioners' sugar. Store, covered, in the refrigerator or freezer.

MAKES ABOUT 30 SMALL BARS

POHA BERRY STRUDEL

I was introduced to poha berries when I first came to Maui, where they grow wild. Mainlanders call them Cape gooseberries. They are not very plentiful, so we're lucky to get a pretty consistent supply from our friend chef Amy Ferguson-Ota on the Island of Hawai'i. You can get them fresh from New Zealand, too. They resemble small tomatillos before they are removed from their husks. If you can't find poha berries or Cape gooseberries, you can substitute cranberries, but you'll have to add an extra cup or so of sugar. I prefer my strudel served warm with a little bit of raspberry sauce (page 184) and vanilla ice cream. — T.G.

8 (4-inch) squares frozen puff pastry

POHA BERRY COMPOTE

2 cups fresh or frozen poha berries
1 cup sugar
1 tablespoon water
$1/4$ cup plus 2 tablespoons cornstarch

2 egg yolks
1 tablespoon water

Place the puff pastry in the refrigerator to thaw overnight.

To prepare the compote, if using frozen berries, set them out to thaw. In a saucepan, mix 1 cup of the thawed berries with the sugar. Let this sit with no heat until it starts to form a juice. This should take about 1 hour. Turn the heat on low and bring to a boil.

Meanwhile, in a bowl, stir together the water and cornstarch. Add the cornstarch mixture to the boiling liquid along with the remaining 1 cup berries. Bring back to a boil, stirring from the bottom, and cook for 10 minutes, just until the mixture thickens. Let cool completely before filling the puff pastry.

In a small bowl, whisk together the egg yolks and water to form an egg wash. Fold a puff pastry square in half on the diagonal to form a triangle. Lay back out flat. Choose 1 of the triangular halves of the square to be the top of your strudel. Cut through this half of the dough in parallel diagonal lines going from the fold to the outer edges, stopping $1/2$ inch away from the edges. Turn over and brush the edges of the uncut side with egg wash. Spoon in 2 tablespoons of the berry filling. Fold the cut half of the dough over the filling, press down, and seal shut with your fingertips so it resembles a turnover. Place on an ungreased baking sheet. Repeat, using the remaining berries and pastry squares to make 8 strudels in all. Cover and refrigerate for 30 minutes.

Preheat the oven to 400°. Brush the egg wash on the strudels. Bake for 20 minutes, until puffed and golden brown. Remove from the oven and serve warm.

SERVES 8

🌿 I make my own puff pastry, but it's a very labor-intensive process. For this recipe you can use frozen puff pastry squares. I recommend the Pepperidge Farm brand.

Oh. You thought the crab dip recipe was going to be in *THIS* chapter? Sorry. Not here.

Winter Recipes to Warm the Heart

I knew of and admired painter Jan Kasprzycki's work before I met him. Then my friend Tom Faught introduced us and a new artistic friendship was established. I quickly became one of Jan and his

wife Kathy's favorite chefs. Because most of Jan's work is extremely large in scale, the wide open spaces of the store made it a natural venue for his art. He always occupies—with one great big canvas—the wall to the right of the entrance door. He changes the painting with each season. We've exhibited some amazing artwork in that space, most notably the "Poinsettias" that goes up with the Christmas tree every year and has become an essential part of our holiday celebrations. 🌺

CURRIED LAMB WONTONS WITH APRICOT DIPPING SAUCE

At parties when I need a one-bite item, I like using wonton skins with different fillings to make "pass pupus." I stuff them with savory, unusual fillings that often result from having delicious leftovers. We serve these lamb-stuffed gems with an apricot sauce for dipping.

APRICOT DIPPING SAUCE

1/2 cup apricot jam

1/2 cup Chinese plum sauce

1 tablespoon rice vinegar

2 teaspoons Dijon mustard

FILLING

1 teaspoon olive oil

2 teaspoons Asian sesame oil

1/2 cup finely chopped onion

1/2 cup peeled and finely chopped carrot

1 tablespoon peeled and finely chopped fresh ginger

1 teaspoon finely chopped garlic

1 tablespoon plus 1 1/2 teaspoons soy sauce

2 tablespoons sesame seeds, toasted (page 63)

2 1/2 teaspoons yellow curry powder, or to taste

1/2 teaspoon salt

1/2 teaspoon freshly ground black pepper

2 cups finely chopped or ground cooked lamb

2 tablespoons cornstarch

2 tablespoons water

1 package (3-inch-square) wonton skins (about 30 skins)

Peanut oil, for deep-frying

To prepare the dipping sauce, in a small bowl, combine all the ingredients and mix well. Set aside.

To prepare the filling, in a saucepan, heat the olive and sesame oils over medium heat. Add the onion, carrot, ginger, and garlic and sauté for 4 minutes, until the vegetables are limp. Add the soy sauce, sesame seeds, curry powder, salt, and pepper. Remove from the heat.

Place the lamb in a bowl, add the cooked vegetable mixture, and mix well. Adjust the seasoning.

To assemble the wontons, in a small bowl, stir together the cornstarch and water. Lay out 6 to 8 wonton skins, positioning each of them with a point facing you. Put about 1 tablespoon of the filling in the center of 1 skin. Brush the edges of the skin with the cornstarch mixture. Fold the bottom edge up to the top edge, covering the filling, and pressing the edges together to seal. You'll have a triangle. Fold the two lower sides of the triangle together and press to seal. Repeat this procedure until you've used all the filling. Cover and chill for a few hours before frying.

In a heavy saucepan, pour in the peanut oil to a depth of about 1 inch and heat to 375°. Add the wontons, a few at a time, and fry, turning with tongs to fry evenly, for about 1 minute, until golden brown. Using a slotted spoon, transfer to paper towels to drain. Serve hot with the dipping sauce.

SERVES 8

DUCK SPRING ROLLS
WITH MANGO DIPPING SAUCE

I demonstrate this recipe a lot. It teaches home cooks a technique that is useful for making many roll-based recipes. You only have to roll three hundred or so before you get very good and quick at it.

FILLING

3 cups cooked and shredded duck (page 13)

1 carrot, peeled and shredded

2 cups shredded green cabbage

4 green onions, white and green parts, finely chopped

3 cloves garlic, finely chopped

1 tablespoon peeled and grated fresh ginger

1/2 teaspoon salt

1/4 cup finely chopped fresh cilantro

1 tablespoon Asian sesame oil

2 teaspoons Vietnamese garlic-chile sauce

1 tablespoon oyster sauce

2 tablespoons sesame seeds, toasted (page 63)

2 tablespoons cornstarch

2 tablespoons water

16 to 18 spring roll wrappers

Peanut oil, for deep-frying

MANGO DIPPING SAUCE

4 shallots, chopped

1/4 cup dry white wine

1/2 cup duck jus or chicken stock (see page 10)

1/2 cup Dijon mustard

1/2 cup puréed mango chutney

1/2 cup heavy cream

To prepare the filling, in a large bowl, combine all the ingredients and mix well.

To assemble the spring rolls, in a small bowl, stir together the cornstarch and water. Lay out 6 spring roll wrappers, positioning each of them with a point facing you. Place 2 heaping tablespoons of the filling across the bottom of 1 wrapper, about 2 inches above the point. Fold the bottom up over the filling and fold in the sides toward the middle. Put a dab of the cornstarch mixture on the top point. Starting at the bottom, roll up to form a tidy bundle. Repeat with the remaining filling and wrappers. Cover and chill for at least 1 hour before frying.

To prepare the sauce, in a small saucepan, combine the shallots, wine, and duck jus and place over medium heat. Cook for 6 to 8 minutes, until reduced to 1/2 cup. Add the mustard, chutney, and cream and cook for 4 to 5 minutes, until thick. Pour into a bowl and set aside.

In a heavy saucepan, pour in the peanut oil to a depth of about 1 inch and heat to 375°. Add 2 spring rolls and fry, turning with tongs to fry evenly, for 1 1/2 to 2 minutes, until crisp and browned. Using tongs or a wire skimmer, transfer to paper towels to drain. Repeat with the remaining rolls. Serve hot with the dipping sauce.

_____

SERVES 8

KĀLUA PORK AND GOAT CHEESE QUESADILLAS

It's the delicious fatty taste from the kālua pork and richness of the goat cheese that make this dish a true taste sensation. I'm going to tell you how to simulate kālua pork at home, but if you have a relative or a friend in Hawai'i, get them to send you the real thing. Or, given today's technology, you might check out kaluapig.com.

INSTANT KĀLUA PORK

1 (3-pound) pork butt, cut in half
Salt
Freshly ground black pepper
1 tablespoon liquid smoke
3 cups water

1 tablespoon olive oil
1 cup chopped onion
16 (6-inch) flour tortillas (page 72)
¹/2 pound fresh goat cheese
2 tablespoons chopped fresh chives
1 tablespoon Asian sesame oil
Avocado salsa (page 72)
Spicy cherry tomato salad (page 72)

To prepare the pork, preheat the oven to 325°. Place the pork butt in a roasting pan and season to taste with salt and pepper. Add the liquid smoke and water to the pan. Cover tightly with aluminum foil. Cook for 2 hours, until the pork is very tender and almost falling apart. Transfer the pork to a platter. Let cool and then shred the pork. Measure out 2 cups. Reserve the remainder for another use.

In a skillet, heat the olive oil over medium heat. Add the onion, decrease the heat to low, and cook, stirring, for 20 minutes, until caramelized. Remove from the heat.

Lay out 8 of the tortillas. Spread a light coating of goat cheese on each of them. Divide the 2 cups pork evenly among the tortillas, spooning it in an even layer. Divide the caramelized onion evenly among the tortillas. Sprinkle evenly with the chives. Top each tortilla with a second tortilla and press together. Brush one side with sesame oil.

Heat a nonstick skillet over medium-high heat. When it is hot, place a quesadilla, oil side down, in the pan. Fry for 2 to 3 minutes, until golden brown. Brush the top side with sesame oil, flip it over, and fry for 1 to 2 minutes longer, until golden brown. Transfer to a cutting board and keep warm. Repeat with the rest of the quesadillas.

Cut each quesadilla into 6 wedges and serve hot with the salsa and salad.

SERVES 8

FISH CAKES WITH
WASABI-GINGER TARTAR SAUCE

Instead of crab cakes, which you see on so many menus, we do fish cakes. It is a great way to use up those small ends of fresh fish fillets. Just about any combination of fish will do. We usually use mahi, snapper, ahi, halibut, and sea bass.

WASABI-GINGER TARTAR SAUCE

2 cups good-quality mayonnaise

1 tablespoon wasabi paste

2 tablespoons pickled chopped ginger

1 tablespoon peeled and minced fresh ginger

1/4 cup finely chopped red onion

4 cloves garlic, finely chopped

3 tablespoons chopped fresh cilantro

2 teaspoons freshly squeezed lime juice

FISH CAKES

1 pound assorted fish fillets, finely chopped

1/4 cup finely chopped green onion, white part only

1/4 cup seeded and finely chopped red bell pepper

1 teaspoon finely chopped garlic

2 tablespoons finely chopped fresh basil

1 tablespoon finely chopped fresh cilantro

1/2 cup good-quality mayonnaise

2 eggs, lightly beaten

2 teaspoons salt

1/2 teaspoon freshly ground black pepper

2 cups panko (Japanese bread crumbs)

1/2 cup peanut oil

Lime slices, for garnish

Cucumber slices, for garnish

To prepare the sauce, in a small bowl, mix together the mayonnaise and wasabi paste until well blended. Add the remaining sauce ingredients and mix well. Set aside.

To prepare the cakes, in a bowl, combine all the ingredients and mix well. Form into cakes about 2 1/2 inches in diameter and 1/2 inch thick. You should have 6 cakes. Coat the cakes evenly with the panko, cover, and chill for 1 hour.

In a skillet, heat the oil over medium-high heat. In batches, add the cakes and fry, turning once, for 2 1/2 to 3 minutes on each side, until golden brown.

To serve, place a fish cake atop a pool of tartar sauce on each plate. Garnish with lime and cucumber slices.

SERVES 6

SEARED FOIE GRAS
WITH SPICY MANGO SAUCE

I'm known for my passion for foie gras. At a dinner cooked by Michael Ginor, the owner of New York's Hudson Valley Foie Gras, I was presented with a serving platter full of foie gras for my main course. I don't think there's anything better than a perfectly seared "extra-large" piece of this heavenly food paired with a tropical fruit. Garnishing it with fried Maui onions makes it even better.

1¹/2 pounds fresh foie gras

1 tablespoon olive oil

2 tablespoons peeled and minced ginger

2 cloves garlic, minced

1 cup diced mango

¹/2 cup pineapple juice

2 tablespoons freshly squeezed lime juice

¹/4 teaspoon Vietnamese garlic-chile sauce

Salt

Freshly ground black pepper

Working quickly so the foie gras remains chilled, carefully pull apart the lobes with your hands and cut or pull out the connective tissue. Slice on the diagonal into 1/2-inch-thick slices. Place on a piece of parchment paper and refrigerate for 1 hour, until well chilled.

In a small saucepan, heat the olive oil over medium heat. Add the ginger and garlic and sauté for 1 minute, until softened. Add the mango, pineapple juice, lime juice, and chile sauce and simmer for 4 to 5 minutes, until the mango breaks down and the liquid is almost evaporated. Transfer the mango mixture to a blender and purée. Set aside.

Heat a nonstick sauté pan over high heat until very hot. Season the foie gras with salt and pepper. Add the foie gras slices to the pan and sear for 30 to 40 seconds on each side, until browned.

To serve, place a pool of the mango sauce in the center of each plate. Top each with 2 slices of foie gras.

SERVES 8

TOMATO AND WILD RICE SOUP

I once had quite a bit of cooked wild rice left over from a party we'd catered. I refused to throw away good rice and this recipe was the result. A rustic soup like this one is welcomed by our guests during winter.

4 tablespoons unsalted butter

1 cup chopped onion

1 cup peeled and chopped carrot

$1/2$ cup chopped celery

4 shallots, minced

$4^1/2$ cups chicken stock (see page 10)

1 (28-ounce) can crushed tomatoes with purée

2 cups cooked wild rice

1 teaspoon sugar

2 tablespoons chopped fresh thyme

1 teaspoon salt

$1/2$ teaspoon freshly ground black pepper

In a heavy saucepan, melt the butter over medium-high heat. Add the onion, carrot, celery, and shallots and sauté for 8 to 10 minutes, until the vegetables are limp. Add the stock and tomatoes and simmer for 10 minutes. Add the rice, sugar, and thyme and heat through. Season with salt and pepper. To serve, ladle the soup into warmed shallow soup bowls.

SERVES 8

SEAFOOD CHOWDER

How can you not have a seafood chowder on the menu when you're in the middle of the Pacific? All the fresh fish you could possibly want to eat is easy to get right here.

6 slices bacon, finely chopped

1 onion, finely chopped

4 cups peeled and diced potatoes

3 cups rich seafood stock (see page 10)

6 tablespoons unsalted butter

4 cups cubed mild fish fillet

2 tablespoons flour, seasoned with salt and freshly ground black pepper

2 cups corn kernels (from about 4 ears)

1 cup heavy cream

1 teaspoon sugar

1 cup half-and-half

1/4 teaspoon white pepper

Salt

In a large saucepan, sauté the bacon over medium heat for about 3 minutes, until crisp. Add the onion and cook for 2 minutes, until softened. Add the potatoes and stock, cover, and simmer for about 15 minutes, until the potatoes are tender.

Meanwhile, in a sauté pan, melt 4 tablespoons of the butter over medium-high heat. Toss the fish cubes in the seasoned flour and add to the pan. Sauté for about 2 minutes, until just cooked through. Set aside.

When the potatoes are tender, add the corn, cream, sugar, and remaining 2 tablespoons of butter. Add the fish and simmer for 3 to 4 minutes, until heated through. Add the half-and-half and simmer another 5 minutes, until hot. Add the pepper and salt to taste. To serve, ladle into warmed individual soup bowls.

SERVES 6

GARLIC-POTATO SOUP

With the exception of the Seafood Chowder (opposite page), we get more requests for this soup than any other. People will actually call the restaurant to ask what the soup of the day is, and if it's this one, you can bet they'll come through the door at lunch. I find it amusing because it's so simple to make.

7 tablespoons unsalted butter, at room
   temperature

1 large yellow onion, coarsely chopped

2 heads garlic (about 30 cloves total), crushed

4 cups peeled and cut-up potatoes (1/2-inch pieces)

6 cups rich chicken stock (see page 10)

1 tablespoon chopped fresh thyme

1 teaspoon salt

1/2 teaspoon freshly ground black pepper

1/2 cup heavy cream

In a Dutch oven or large pot, melt 3 tablespoons of the butter over medium heat. Add the onion and garlic and sauté for 5 minutes, until the onion is translucent. Add the potatoes, stock, thyme, salt, and pepper and bring to a boil. Decrease the heat to low and simmer, uncovered, for about 25 minutes, until the potatoes are tender.

Drain the soup, reserving the liquid. Let cool slightly, then, in batches, purée the solids in a blender, adding some of the reserved liquid as needed to ease the blending. Place the purée back in the pot. Add the reserved liquid and stir in the cream. Place over low heat and heat for 2 minutes, until warmed to serving temperature. Adjust the seasoning. To serve, ladle into warmed individual soup bowls.

SERVES 8

PORTUGUESE BEAN SOUP

Every local family in Hawai'i has its own version of Portuguese bean soup. One Christmas, our book-keeper, Patrice Tuzon, gave us a big container filled with a batch made according to her family recipe, and now it's my favorite. With her aloha, it's included here. She says, "It's all in the sausage," and the brand she uses is No Ka Oi (hot) from Ah Fook's supermarket—a very appropriate choice since no ka oi *is Hawaiian for "the very best."*

2 smoked ham hocks

3 or 4 Portuguese sausages (linguiça)

1 (8-ounce) can tomato sauce

4 (15-ounce) cans kidney beans, drained and rinsed

2 or 3 medium carrots, peeled and sliced

2 large white or red potatoes, peeled and cubed

2 medium-sized sweet potatoes, peeled and cubed

1 bunch watercress, chopped

$^1/_2$ teaspoon ground cinnamon

1 teaspoon sugar

$^3/_4$ cup ketchup

8 sprigs watercress, for garnish

In a large saucepan, combine the ham hocks, sausages, and tomato sauce. Add water to cover by about 3 inches and place over medium-high heat. Bring to a boil, and continue to boil for 20 minutes. Remove the sausages and set aside.

Decrease the heat to medium, cover, and cook the ham hocks for about 40 minutes, until tender. Remove the ham hocks from the pot. When cool enough to handle, remove the bones and fat from the ham hocks and cut the meat into chunks.

Add the kidney beans to the pan and cook for 10 minutes. Add the carrots and potatoes and continue to cook for about 25 minutes, until they are tender and the soup begins to thicken.

Slice the sausages and add them and the watercress to the soup. Add the ham hock meat, the cinnamon, sugar, and ketchup and simmer until the sausages are heated through. To serve, ladle the soup into individual soup crocks and garnish with the watercress sprigs.

SERVES 8

GRILLED QUAIL SALAD WITH CRISPY ONION STRINGS AND TOASTED MACADAMIA NUTS

I'm asked to do numerous sit-down dinner events, such as dining-under-the-stars for two, or "bring the restaurant" to the eighteenth hole of a golf course for thirty. These events provide a creative outlet outside the restaurant. This dish was created for one of those evenings. It gets added to the restaurant menu at Christmastime.

QUAIL

1/2 teaspoon finely chopped garlic

1 teaspoon chopped fresh cilantro

1 teaspoon peeled and finely chopped fresh ginger

1 teaspoon finely chopped lemongrass, white part only

1/2 cup extra virgin olive oil

Salt

Freshly ground black pepper

6 boneless quails

MANGO CHUTNEY VINAIGRETTE

1/2 cup mango chutney

2 tablespoons Dijon mustard

2 teaspoons chopped chipotle chile in adobo

1/2 teaspoon sugar

1 tablespoon freshly squeezed lime juice

1/2 cup canola oil

2 tablespoons rice vinegar

Pinch of salt

CRISPY ONION STRINGS

1 onion, thinly sliced

Flour seasoned with salt, freshly ground black pepper, and cayenne pepper

Peanut oil, for deep-frying

1 pineapple, peeled, cut into 8 (1/2-inch) slices, and cored

Olive oil, for brushing

6 cups mixed baby salad greens

1/4 cup macadamia nut pieces, toasted (page 106), for garnish

2 tablespoons chopped fresh chives, for garnish

To prepare the quail, in a shallow container, mix together the garlic, cilantro, ginger, lemongrass, olive oil, and salt and pepper to taste. Add the quail, cover, and marinate in the refrigerator overnight.

Prepare a fire in a charcoal grill, or preheat a gas grill.

To prepare the vinaigrette, in a small bowl, mix together the chutney, mustard, chile, sugar, and lime juice. Whisk in the oil, vinegar, and salt and blend until smooth. Set aside.

To prepare the onions, in a bowl, add the onion slices to the flour. Toss to coat, then shake off the excess. In a heavy saucepan, pour in the oil to a depth of 2 inches and heat to 375°. Fry the onions, in batches, for 3 minutes, until crispy. Using a wire skimmer, transfer to paper towels to drain, and keep warm.

Place the quail on the grill rack and grill, turning once, for 4 minutes on each side, until golden brown. Brush the pineapple slices with olive oil and place on the grill. Cook, turning once, for about 3 minutes on each side, until warmed through but not overcooked.

To assemble each salad, place a pineapple slice in the center of each plate. Reserve 6 tablespoons of the vinaigrette. Toss the greens with the remaining vinaigrette. Place 1 cup of the greens on the plate to half cover the pineapple. Place a quail on top of the greens. Top the quail with onion strings. Drizzle 1 tablespoon of the reserved vinaigrette on each serving. Sprinkle the macadamia nuts and chives around the plate.

SERVES 6

WHITE BEAN, GOAT CHEESE,
AND ROASTED VEGETABLE SALAD

A lot of vegetarians come through our doors, so I'm always looking for new ways to use our bounty of fresh vegetables. I created this salad during my "white period."

WHITE BEANS

*1 rounded cup (¹/2 pound) dried small
    white beans*

2 tablespoons olive oil

2 tablespoons finely chopped onion

2 tablespoons finely chopped celery

2 tablespoons peeled and finely chopped carrot

5 sprigs thyme

4 cups chicken stock (see page 10)

Salt

Freshly ground black pepper

Extra virgin olive oil, for binding

ROASTED VEGETABLES

2 globe eggplants, sliced ¹/4 inch thick

2 zucchini, sliced ¹/4 inch thick

2 tablespoons extra virgin olive oil

Salt

Freshly ground black pepper

LEMON VINAIGRETTE

¹/4 cup freshly squeezed lemon juice

²/3 cup extra virgin olive oil

1 tablespoon Dijon mustard

Salt

Freshly ground black pepper

2 teaspoons chopped fresh thyme

³/4 pound fresh goat cheese, at room temperature

3 cups mixed salad greens

To prepare the beans, pick them over, rinse, and place in a bowl with water to cover. Let soak overnight. Drain and set aside.

In a saucepan, heat the olive oil over medium-low heat. Add the onion, celery, and carrot and sauté for 5 minutes, until tender. Add the beans, thyme, and stock. Bring to a boil over high heat, and skim off any foam. Decrease the heat to low and simmer, uncovered, for 30 to 45 minutes, until the beans are tender but not falling apart. Remove from the heat. Drain the beans well, place in a bowl, and season with salt and pepper.

Transfer one-half of the beans to a separate bowl and mash with a potato masher. Add the mashed beans to the whole beans and mix gently together, adding a small amount of extra virgin olive oil to help bind all the beans together. Set aside.

To prepare the vegetables, place the eggplant slices in a colander and salt them. Let drain for 30 minutes.

Preheat the oven to 400°. Brush the eggplant and zucchini with oil and sprinkle with salt and pepper. Place the vegetables on a nonstick baking sheet and roast for 5 minutes, then turn over and roast for 3 minutes longer, until browned and tender. When cool, cut the eggplant and zucchini into ¹/4-inch cubes. Set aside.

Combine all the vinaigrette ingredients except the thyme in a blender and process until emulsified. Add the thyme.

Line a baking sheet with parchment paper. Divide the goat cheese into 6 equal portions. Form each portion into a circle 3 inches in diameter. Place on the baking sheet and chill well.

Preheat the oven to 350°. Spray 6 (8-ounce) glass bowls with vegetable-oil cooking spray. Place ¹/2 cup of the grilled vegetables in each prepared bowl and press down. Place 1 piece of the goat cheese on top of the vegetables. Spoon ¹/2 cup of the beans onto each piece of cheese and press down. Bake the molds for 10 to 12 minutes, until slightly browned. Remove from the oven.

Toss the salad greens with the vinaigrette. To compose each salad, place ¹/2 cup of the dressed greens in the middle of each plate. Invert a vegetable mold on top of the greens and carefully lift the bowl from around the baked mixture. Serve immediately.

SERVES 6

SEARED BEEF SALAD

I created this dish for a cooking class to illustrate how to use some of the Islands' unusual ingredients, from soba noodles to wasabi to hoisin sauce. You can take the basic ingredients and techniques and use ahi tuna or chicken instead of beef, and dried rice noodles instead of soba noodles. I made this salad on the Today Show *and Matt, Katie, and Al loved it!*

MARINADE

1 tablespoon peeled and minced fresh ginger

1 tablespoon minced garlic

1/4 cup soy sauce

1/2 cup hoisin sauce

1/4 cup sake

1 tablespoon plus 1 1/2 teaspoons sugar

1 pound well-trimmed New York steak,
    cut into 1/2-inch strips

Salt

Freshly ground black pepper

2 tablespoons Asian sesame oil

STIR-FRY VEGETABLES

1 tablespoon olive oil

1/4 cup peeled and shredded carrot

1/2 cup thinly sliced Maui onion

1/2 cup sugar snap peas

1/2 cup sliced shiitake mushrooms

1/2 cup bean sprouts

2 tablespoons minced garlic

1 tablespoon peeled and minced fresh ginger

1/2 cup shredded won bok (Chinese cabbage)

1/2 cup pear tomatoes, stemmed

2 tablespoons fresh mint leaves

2 tablespoons fresh cilantro leaves

NOODLE CAKES

1 pound dried soba noodles

2 tablespoons Asian sesame oil

1 cup peanut oil

WASABI VINAIGRETTE

3 tablespoons rice vinegar

1 tablespoon soy sauce

3/4 cup olive oil

1 tablespoon wasabi paste

1 teaspoon white miso paste

1 teaspoon ground toasted sesame seeds (page 63)

4 handfuls mixed baby salad greens

Toasted macadamia nut pieces (page 106), for garnish

To prepare the marinade, in a shallow nonreactive pan, combine all the ingredients. Add the steak strips, cover, and marinate in the refrigerator overnight.

The next day, remove the meat from the marinade and season with salt and pepper.

In a heavy sauté pan, heat the sesame oil over high heat. Add the meat and cook, turning once, for about 2 minutes on each side for medium rare. Transfer the meat to a plate and keep warm.

To prepare the vegetables, add the olive oil to the same pan over high heat. In 30-second intervals, add the vegetables in the following order: carrot, onion, peas, mushrooms, sprouts, garlic, ginger, cabbage, and tomatoes. After the tomatoes are added, stir-fry for 1 minute longer, then stir in the mint and cilantro. The vegetables should remain crisp. Remove from the heat and set aside.

To prepare the noodle cakes, bring a saucepan filled with water to a boil. Add the soba noodles and boil for 6 to 7 minutes, until al dente. Drain and toss with the sesame oil. Divide the noodles into 4 equal portions, and form each into a cake.

Heat a 6-inch heavy skillet over high heat and add the peanut oil. Continue heating until the oil is smoking. Add one portion of the noodles and fry for about 2 minutes, until browned on the first side. Carefully flip the noodle cake over and fry for 2 to 3 minutes longer, until cooked on the second side. Using a slotted spoon, transfer to paper towels to drain. Repeat with the remaining noodles. Keep warm.

To prepare the vinaigrette, combine all the ingredients in a blender and blend until smooth. To assemble the salads, place a noodle cake in the center of each plate. Top with a handful of salad greens. Place one-fourth of the stir-fried vegetables on each mound of salad greens, and top with one-fourth of the beef. Drizzle with the vinaigrette and sprinkle with macadamia nuts. Serve immediately.

SERVES 4

🌸 You must mix wasabi powder with water to form a paste before using it. Never just add the powder.

If you decide to use rice noodles, you will need to deep-fry them. In a heavy saucepan, pour in peanut oil to a depth of 2 inches and heat to 375°. Break the noodles apart (it is best to do this with scissors). Drop them by handfuls into the hot oil. The noodles will immediately crisp up. Flip them once, remove them from the oil, and drain on paper towels.

Fettuccine with Gorgonzola Sauce

This is a simple pasta dish, in both method of preparation and in flavors. Serve it as a quick and hearty winter main course.

2 tablespoons unsalted butter

$^1/_2$ cup peeled and finely chopped carrot

$^1/_2$ cup finely chopped celery

1 shallot, peeled and finely chopped

1 clove garlic, chopped

4 cups heavy cream

$^1/_4$ cup grated Parmesan cheese

$^1/_4$ cup shredded Gruyère cheese

Salt

Freshly ground black pepper

8 ounces Gorgonzola cheese, diced

4 tablespoons extra virgin olive oil

1 pound fresh fettuccine

Chopped fresh flat-leaf parsley, for garnish

$^1/_2$ cup toasted pecan halves (page 106), for garnish

$^1/_2$ cup julienned oil-packed sundried tomatoes, for garnish

In a large saucepan, melt the butter over medium heat. Add the carrot, celery, shallot, and garlic and sauté for 2 minutes, until tender. Add the cream and cook for 10 minutes, until reduced by one-third. Decrease the heat to low, add the Parmesan and Gruyère cheeses, and season with salt and pepper. Mix well, stir in the Gorgonzola, and continue to cook for 2 to 3 minutes, stirring frequently to prevent burning.

Meanwhile, bring a large saucepan filled with water to a boil. Add 2 tablespoons of the olive oil and the fettuccine, stir well, and cook for 2 minutes, until al dente.

Drain the fettuccine well, coat with the remaining 2 tablespoons olive oil, add it to the sauce, and toss well. Turn the pasta and sauce into a large warmed serving bowl. Sprinkle with the parsley, pecans, and sundried tomatoes. Serve immediately.

Serves 4

BAKED CHICKEN WITH WHITE BEANS AND ROASTED VEGETABLE RAGOUT

Contrary to popular belief, it does get chilly in upcountry Maui. There's nothing better than this stick-to-your ribs, soul-warming dish in winter.

WHITE BEANS

2 cups small dried white beans

3 cups chicken stock (see page 10)

1/4 cup cider vinegar

1/2 cup peeled and finely chopped carrot

2 celery stalks, finely chopped

1/4 cup finely chopped onion

1 bay leaf

1 sprig thyme

1/2 teaspoon salt

1/4 teaspoon freshly ground black pepper

MARINADE

2 shallots, finely chopped

3 cloves garlic

1/4 cup chopped fresh basil

1/4 cup chopped fresh cilantro

1 cup extra virgin olive oil

Juice of 2 lemons

1/4 teaspoon salt

1/4 teaspoon freshly ground black pepper

6 boneless chicken breast halves, skin on

ROASTED VEGETABLE RAGOUT

2 red bell peppers, seeded and diced

4 tomatoes, coarsely chopped

1/2 cup diced leek, white part only

1 large onion, diced

1 globe eggplant, diced

1 tablespoon olive oil

6 sprigs thyme

8 cloves garlic, minced

Salt

Freshly ground black pepper

To prepare the beans, pick them over, rinse well, and place in a bowl with water to cover. Let soak overnight.

The next day, prepare the marinade: Combine all the ingredients in a food processor or blender and purée until smooth. Place the chicken pieces in a shallow nonreactive container, pour the marinade over the top, and turn the chicken to coat evenly. Cover and marinate in the refrigerator for 2 hours.

Drain the beans. In a heavy saucepan, combine the beans, stock, vinegar, carrot, celery, onion, bay leaf, and thyme. Bring to a boil over high heat and skim off any foam. Lower the heat to medium and simmer, covered, for 30 to 45 minutes, until the beans are tender. If the beans soak up too much liquid before they are tender, add a little water to prevent scorching. Season with salt and pepper, set aside, and keep warm.

To prepare the chicken, preheat the oven to 375°. Remove the chicken from the marinade and place in a roasting pan. Bake for 25 to 30 minutes, until golden brown. Remove from the oven, leaving the oven on, and keep warm until serving.

To make the vegetable ragout, in a large bowl, combine the bell peppers, tomatoes, leek, onion, and eggplant. Drizzle with the olive oil and add the thyme sprigs and garlic. Toss to coat well. Season with salt and pepper and toss again. Transfer to a roasting pan, spreading the mixture in an even layer, and roast for 20 to 25 minutes, until tender. Keep warm until serving.

To assemble each serving, place one-sixth of the beans in the center of each plate. Place one piece of chicken on top of the beans, and cover the chicken with one-sixth of the vegetable ragout. Serve at once.

SERVES 6

Pine Nut–Crusted Opakapaka
with Garlic-Tomato-Dill Beurre Blanc

You'll notice that many of our fish recipes have crusts. In addition to being tasty, the crust seals in the juices and ensures that every bite, even in a well-done preparation, will be moist. Opakapaka is a deep-water, line-fished pink snapper and one of Hawai'i's most popular fishes. It doesn't taste like any snapper caught anywhere else in the world.

1/4 cup pine nuts

1 1/2 cups panko (Japanese bread crumbs) or plain dried bread crumbs

4 (6-ounce) opakapaka fillets

Salt

Freshly ground black pepper

1/2 cup good-quality mayonnaise

2 tablespoons olive oil

3 cloves garlic, finely chopped

1 large tomato, seeded and finely chopped

1 cup dry white wine

Juice of 1 lemon

1 cup (1/2 pound) cold unsalted butter, cut into small pieces

1 tablespoon capers, drained

1 tablespoon plus 1 1/2 teaspoons chopped fresh dill

Lemon slices, for garnish and wedges for serving

Sprigs of dill, for garnish

To prepare the crust, combine the pine nuts and panko in a food processor and process until finely ground. Spread the nut mixture on a plate.

To prepare the fish fillets, lightly season them on one side with salt and pepper and then cover each one on the same side with 2 tablespoons of the mayonnaise. Press the seasoned side of each fillet into the pine nut mixture, coating evenly.

In a large sauté pan, heat the oil over medium heat. Add the fish fillets, crust side down, and sauté for 3 minutes, until light brown. Turn the fish and cook for 2 more minutes, until the fish is barely opaque in the center. Transfer the fish to warmed dinner plates.

Remove any excess crust from the pan and add the garlic and tomato over medium heat. Sauté for 1 minute; do not let the garlic get brown. Add the wine and cook for 5 minutes, until reduced by half. Add the lemon juice, then stir in the cold butter, a few pieces at a time, until the sauce thickens. Do not allow to boil. Stir in the capers and dill.

Spoon the sauce over the fish, garnish with the lemon slices and dill, and serve immediately with the lemon wedges.

Serves 4

✎ You can substitute other snappers, sole, perch, cod, or other whitefish for the opakapaka. If you don't want to use mayonnaise to adhere the crust, you can dip the fillets in a wash of milk and eggs.

ISLAND BOUILLABAISSE

One of my most memorable meals was at Restaurant Tatou in the south of France in 1982. The only entrée served there is bouillabaisse, which has four different kinds of fish. I remember seeing the big pots of broth sitting on the stove and watching the chef ladle the broth over the fish to cook it. This is my version of the memory of that meal, Island style. The pesto can double as a wonderful marinade for grilled steaks and shrimp.

ASIAN FISH STOCK

6 pounds fresh fish bones (no gills or blood lines), coarsely chopped

1 onion, chopped

4 celery stalks, chopped

6 cloves garlic, chopped

1 lemongrass stalk, white part only, pounded

6 shiitake mushrooms, chopped

1 bay leaf

1 bunch thyme

Pinch of saffron

1 teaspoon black peppercorns

2 cups bottled clam juice

2 tomatoes, quartered

2 tablespoons peeled and minced fresh ginger

2 cups dry white wine

4 quarts water

LEMONGRASS-GINGER PESTO

2 lemongrass stalks

8 cloves garlic

1/4 cup peeled and coarsely chopped fresh ginger

1/2 cup chopped fresh cilantro, preferably with roots

1/4 cup canola oil

1/2 teaspoon sambal (Indonesian garlic-chile paste)

MISO BUTTER

2 tablespoons white miso

1/2 cup fresh flat-leaf parsley leaves

3 cloves garlic

4 tablespoons unsalted butter, at room temperature

6 small Yukon Gold potatoes, about 1 pound total

3 tablespoons olive oil

1 cup julienned onion

12 large sea scallops

12 shrimp (about 3/4 pound), peeled and deveined

12 lobster claws, shells cracked open

1/2 pound white fish fillets, cut into 1-inch-wide strips

4 tomatoes, seeded and chopped

1/2 cup dry white wine

2 teaspoons salt

1 teaspoon freshly ground black pepper

2 tablespoons chopped fresh flat-leaf parsley

To prepare the fish stock, in a large saucepan, combine all the ingredients and bring to a simmer over medium heat, skimming off any foam. Cook, uncovered, skimming as needed, for 2 hours, until full flavored. Remove from the heat and strain through a fine-mesh sieve. You should have 6 cups. Set aside.

To prepare the pesto, peel off the outer layers off the lemongrass stalks, and coarsely chop the white bulb portion. Place all the pesto ingredients in a food processor and process until smooth.

To prepare the miso butter, combine all the ingredients in a food processor and process until smooth. Set aside.

In a saucepan, combine the potatoes with salted water to

cover, bring to a boil, and cook for 12 to 14 minutes, until cooked through. Drain and allow to cool. Cut in half lengthwise.

In a large saucepan, heat the oil over medium-high heat. Add the onion and sauté for 2 minutes, until wilted. In the following order, add the potatoes, 1 tablespoon of the pesto, the scallops, shrimp, lobster claws, fish, and tomatoes. Add the wine and stir to deglaze, scraping up any browned bits on the pan bottom. Add the salt, pepper, and stock and bring to a simmer over medium heat. Cook for 8 to 10 minutes, until the fish and shellfish are just opaque at the center. Using a wire skimmer, transfer the fish, shellfish, and potatoes to a bowl and keep warm. Increase the heat to high and cook the liquid for 5 minutes, until reduced by one-third. Add the miso butter and the parsley.

Divide the fish, shellfish, and potatoes evenly among warmed bowls. Ladle the stock over each serving and serve immediately.

SERVES 6

🌿 Miso is a soybean paste used frequently in Japanese cooking.

VEGGIE LASAGNA

How many pans of vegetarian lasagna did we serve? Who knows? In its heyday, it was so popular, we put it on the menu at both lunch and dinner, making it one of our biggest-selling items ever. Over the years, the menu became more creative and complex, so we decided to put the veggie lasagna to rest. That was in 1995, and many of our regular customers were dismayed. Now you can all make it yourselves!

MARINARA SAUCE

6 tablespoons olive oil

1/2 cup finely chopped onion

4 cloves garlic, minced

1/4 bulb fennel, finely chopped

1 red bell pepper, seeded and finely diced

1/2 cup peeled and finely chopped carrot

1 (28-ounce) can chopped tomatoes

2 cups tomato sauce

2 tablespoons chopped fresh oregano

2 tablespoons chopped fresh basil

1 1/2 cups dry white wine

1/4 pound mushrooms, chopped

2 teaspoons sugar

1 teaspoon salt

1/2 teaspoon freshly ground black pepper

FILLING

3 cups cooked and chopped spinach

3 cups (1 1/2 pounds) ricotta cheese

1/3 cup grated Parmesan cheese

2 tablespoons chopped fresh basil

2 teaspoons salt

1/2 teaspoon freshly ground black pepper

1 teaspoon ground nutmeg

2 eggs, lightly beaten

2 cups shredded mozzarella cheese

2/3 cup grated Parmesan cheese

1 pound fresh lasagna noodles

To prepare the marinara sauce, in a large, heavy skillet, heat the olive oil over medium heat. Add the onion and garlic and sauté for 5 to 8 minutes, until translucent. Stir in the fennel, bell pepper, carrot, tomatoes, tomato sauce, oregano, basil, and wine and decrease the heat to low. Simmer, uncovered, for 30 to 35 minutes, until thick and chunky. Add the mushrooms, sugar, salt, and pepper. Simmer for 5 minutes longer to blend the flavors. You should have 6 cups.

To prepare the filling, in a bowl, combine the spinach, ricotta and Parmesan cheeses, basil, salt, pepper, nutmeg, and eggs. Mix well.

Preheat the oven to 375°. Spray a 9 by 11-inch baking dish with vegetable-oil cooking spray. In a bowl, mix together the mozzarella and Parmesan cheeses. Generously cover the bottom of the prepared baking dish with 1 cup of the sauce. Add a layer of the noodles and then add 1 cup of the spinach mixture. Top with 1/2 cup of the cheese mixture and then add another 1 cup sauce. Repeat this process for 3 more layers and top with a layer of noodles. Generously sprinkle the final layer of noodles with sauce and the cheese mixture.

Bake for 30 minutes, until bubbly and browned. Let stand for 10 minutes before serving.

SERVES 8 TO 10

✒ You may find this hard believe, but you really don't have to cook the lasagna noodles before baking the dish. If you make sure there's enough sauce on both sides of the noodles, they'll cook just fine with the rest of the dish.

MOUSSAKA

For the first six or eight years we were open, in October—as soon as there was a chill in the air—people would come in and ask, "When's the moussaka going back on the menu?" As with many other dishes, it is now only a memory . . . and a recipe.

4 globe eggplants
Salt
3 tablespoons unsalted butter
3 tablespoons chopped onion
2 teaspoons chopped garlic
1 1/2 pounds ground lamb
1 cup tomato sauce
1/2 cup dry white wine
Freshly ground black pepper
1/2 teaspoon ground cinnamon
1 teaspoon ground nutmeg
1 cup flour
1/2 cup olive oil
2 cups grated Parmesan cheese, for sprinkling
3/4 cup fine dried bread crumbs, for sprinkling

BÉCHAMEL SAUCE

4 cups whole milk
1/3 cup unsalted butter
3/4 cup flour
1 teaspoon salt
1/4 teaspoon freshly ground black pepper
1/2 teaspoon ground nutmeg
2 eggs

✿ Whenever you fry eggplant (except for Asian eggplant), make sure that you salt it well after you slice or dice it. This will remove the excess moisture and any bitterness. After 10 or 15 minutes in a colander, you'll notice a lot of liquid has drained from the eggplant.

Cut the eggplants lengthwise into 1/4-inch-thick slices. You should have around 24 slices. Layer in a large colander, salting each layer, and let drain for 30 minutes.

Meanwhile, prepare the lamb mixture: In a large sauté pan, melt the butter over medium heat. Add the onion and garlic and sauté for 8 to 10 minutes, until lightly browned. Add the ground lamb and sauté for 5 minutes, until browned. Add the tomato sauce, wine, salt and pepper to taste, cinnamon, and nutmeg. Cook the mixture, stirring occasionally, for 4 to 6 minutes, until thickened. Remove from the heat.

Rinse the eggplant and pat dry. Place the flour in a shallow dish and dredge the eggplant slices in it. In a sauté pan, heat the olive oil over high heat. Add the eggplant slices, in batches, and fry, turning once, for about 2 minutes on each side, until golden and tender. Using a slotted spatula or tongs, transfer to paper towels to drain.

To prepare the sauce, heat the milk in a saucepan over medium heat, just until hot. In another saucepan, melt the butter over low heat, until bubbly. Remove from the heat and whisk the flour into the butter. Put the pan back on the heat and cook, stirring, for 1 minute to cook the flour. Slowly add the hot milk to the flour, whisking continuously to prevent lumps. Season with the salt, pepper, and nutmeg. Continue to heat over low heat for about 5 minutes, until the sauce reduces and thickens. Remove from the heat and let cool. Add the eggs and mix thoroughly.

Preheat the oven to 350°. Spray a 9 by 11-inch baking dish with vegetable-oil cooking spray. To assemble, arrange a layer of 8 eggplant slices in the prepared dish. Add a layer of lamb mixture. Ladle the béchamel sauce on in a thin layer. Sprinkle with the Parmesan cheese and bread crumbs. Repeat the layering process 2 more times, until all the ingredients have been used, ending with the bread crumbs. Bake for 20 to 30 minutes, until hot, bubbly, and browned on top. Let sit for 5 minutes before cutting into squares and serving.

SERVES 8

BLACKENED AHI WITH SWEET THAI CHILE SAUCE, WASABI GREENS, TOBIKO, AND MASHED POTATOES

HGS CLASSIC

We've had this dish on the menu in one variation or another for a long time. This version has become a classic. There's nothing like a fisherman pulling up to your back door with an eighty-pound ahi caught just hours before. This is the next best thing to heaven.

SWEET THAI CHILE SAUCE

4 cups rice vinegar

1 cup sugar

1/2 cup seeded and finely diced red bell pepper

1/2 cup finely diced red onion

1 tablespoon peeled and chopped fresh ginger

2 tablespoons chopped fresh cilantro or mint

1 teaspoon Sriracha (Thai garlic-chile paste)

MASHED POTATOES

4 large baking potatoes, scrubbed, peeled, and cubed

2 tablespoons milk

4 tablespoons unsalted butter

Salt

White pepper

BLACKENING SEASONING

1 tablespoon cayenne pepper

1 tablespoon freshly ground black pepper

1 tablespoon paprika

1 1/2 teaspoons dried thyme

1 1/2 teaspoons dried oregano

1 tablespoon garlic powder

1 tablespoon onion powder

2 tablespoons salt

6 (6-ounce) ahi (yellowfin) fillets, well chilled

4 tablespoons clarified unsalted butter, melted (see note)

4 cups mesclun

1/4 cup wasabi vinaigrette (page 156)

2 tablespoons tobiko (flying fish roe)

Fresh whole chives, for garnish

To prepare the sauce, in a saucepan, combine the vinegar and sugar over medium-high heat and bring to a boil, stirring to dissolve the sugar. Cook for 35 to 40 minutes, until reduced and syrupy. Combine the remaining ingredients and add to the reduced liquid, stirring well. Remove from the heat and allow to cool. Set aside 3/4 cup to use for this recipe. Store the remainder in an airtight container in the refrigerator for up to 2 weeks.

To prepare the mashed potatoes, in a large pot, combine the potatoes and water to cover over medium-high heat and bring to a boil. Cook for about 15 minutes, until tender. Drain and place in a bowl. Mash with a potato masher, then add the milk and butter and continue mashing until smooth. Season with salt and pepper to taste.

Heat a cast-iron skillet over high heat until the pan stops smoking and ash collects on the pan bottom. This will take 10 to 15 minutes.

To make the seasoning, in a small bowl, stir together all the ingredients. Spread on a plate.

Dip a chilled ahi fillet into the clarified butter and roll in the seasoning. Place in the skillet. Sear, turning once, for 30 to 40 seconds on each side, until the seasoning blackens. The fillet

should still be very rare. Transfer to a plate and repeat with the remaining fillets.

To assemble the dish, in a bowl, toss the greens with the wasabi vinaigrette, then add the tobiko and toss again. Place $^1\!/_2$ cup of the mashed potatoes on each plate. Top the potatoes with the salad greens, dividing evenly. Top the greens with the ahi. Drizzle a little sweet chile sauce over the fish and around the plate. Garnish with the chives. Serve immediately.

SERVES 6

🍃 The process of CLARIFYING BUTTER separates the butterfat from its water and milk. The resulting liquid will keep about three times longer, does not burn, and has a pure clean flavor. In a saucepan, melt small pieces of unsalted butter over medium-low heat without stirring. When completely melted, let simmer for 5 minutes. Skim the white foam off the top. Strain the mixture well—reserving the clear yellow liquid and discarding the milky white substances. In general, $^1\!/_2$ pound of butter will yield $^2\!/_3$ cup clarified butter.

LAMB CANNELLONI

I created this dish for one of my Grand Chefs on Tour appearances, at which I was joined by Dallas chef Dean Fearing. Grand Chefs on Tour is an annual "fantasy cooking camp" at one of Hawai'i's resort hotels. I wanted to do something with a flavorful lamb stock and thought lamb, Roquefort cheese, and spinach sounded like a great combination for a filling. I wrapped it in thin sheets of fresh pasta and served it in a shallow pool of the stock. It takes time to make, but the end result is well worth the effort.

6 (1¹/₂-pound) lamb shanks
Salt
Freshly ground black pepper
3 tablespoons olive oil
2 cloves garlic, minced
2 shallots, minced
2 tablespoons finely chopped onion
2 tablespoons finely chopped celery
2 tablespoons peeled and finely chopped carrot
4 cups veal stock (see page 10)

STOCK

Reserved lamb shank bones
¹/₄ cup peeled and coarsely chopped carrot
¹/₄ cup coarsely chopped onion
¹/₄ cup coarsely chopped celery
¹/₄ cup coarsely chopped leek, white part only
¹/₂ cup chopped plum tomato
2 tablespoons olive oil
Reserved cooking liquid

3 tablespoons olive oil
1¹/₂ pounds spinach, stems removed
¹/₄ cup finely chopped fresh basil
¹/₂ cup crumbled Roquefort cheese
Salt
Freshly ground black pepper
¹/₄ cup pine nuts, toasted (page 106)
8 (5-inch-square) fresh thin pasta sheets
Sprigs of basil, for garnish

To prepare the shanks, season the lamb shanks with salt and pepper. In a heavy Dutch oven, heat the olive oil over medium-high heat. Add the lamb shanks and brown on all sides for 8 to 10 minutes. Remove from the pan. Add the garlic, shallots, onion, celery, and carrot and sauté for 6 to 7 minutes, until the mixture begins to brown.

Add the shanks back into the pan, pour in the veal stock, add water to cover, and bring to a boil. Decrease the heat to low, cover, and simmer for 1¹/₂ to 2 hours, until the shank meat is fork tender.

Remove the shanks and allow to cool. Pull the meat off 4 of the bones and shred it, leaving the meat on 2 of the bones. Set the shredded meat aside. Save all 6 of the shank bones for the stock. Strain the cooking liquid and set aside.

Preheat the oven to 450°. To prepare the stock, in a heavy Dutch oven, combine the 6 shank bones, carrot, onion, celery, leek, and tomato. Add the olive oil and toss well. Roast in the oven for 12 to 15 minutes, until the shank bones and vegetables are well browned. Remove from the oven and place on the stove top over medium heat. Add the reserved strained cooking liquid along with enough water to cover all the ingredients. Bring to a boil, cover, reduce the heat to low, and simmer for 1¹/₂ hours. Remove from the heat, lift out and discard the shank bones, and strain the stock through a sieve lined with cheesecloth. Return the stock to the pan, place over high heat, and boil until reduced to 3 cups.

In a large skillet, heat 2 tablespoons of the olive oil over medium-high heat. Add the spinach and sauté for 3 minutes, until limp. Let cool, place in a clean kitchen towel, and wring to remove all excess moisture. Chop the spinach.

(continued)

Place the shredded lamb in a bowl. Mix in the spinach, chopped basil, Roquefort cheese, and salt and pepper to taste. Add 3 tablespoons of the pine nuts to the mixture and mix well.

Bring a large pot filled with salted water to a boil. Add the pasta and boil for 2 minutes, until half cooked. Carefully remove the pasta from the water and lightly oil with the remaining 1 tablespoon olive oil. Place flat on parchment or waxed paper and, if not using immediately, cover with plastic wrap to prevent drying.

Preheat the oven to 325°. Spray a 9 by 11-inch baking dish with vegetable-oil cooking spray. Divide the lamb mixture into 8 equal portions. Working with 1 pasta sheet at a time, place a portion of the lamb in a line on the bottom edge. Carefully roll up the pasta, enclosing the lamb fully, and place the roll seam side down in the prepared baking dish. Repeat with the remaining lamb and pasta sheets.

Add enough lamb stock to cover the bottom of the baking dish lightly. Cover the dish tightly with aluminum foil and bake for 12 to 15 minutes, until heated through.

Just before the cannelloni are ready, heat the additional stock in a saucepan on the stove. To assemble each serving, carefully transfer 2 cannelloni to the center of each shallow soup bowl and ladle about 3/4 cup of the hot stock over the top. Garnish with fresh basil and serve immediately.

SERVES 4

BRAISED LAMB SHANKS
WITH BLACK BEAN—TOMATO SAUCE

When I was growing up, my mother would spend months looking for the biggest shanks she could find. When she had six or eight in the freezer, she'd cook them for my father and he'd eat them all. He'd give little tastes to the kids. We didn't really know what they were, but I knew I liked them. I always try to make them around Christmastime. And I'm the same way my mother was: I wait until I can get the really plump, good shanks. My favorite way to serve them is with some good corn bread.

4 large lamb shanks

Salt

Freshly ground black pepper

2 tablespoons peanut oil

1 cup all-purpose flour seasoned with salt
   and pepper

2 cloves garlic, smashed

$^1/_2$ cup coarsely chopped celery

$^1/_2$ cup peeled and coarsely chopped carrot

$^1/_2$ cup coarsely chopped onion

8 cups chicken stock or lamb stock
   (see page 10)

BLACK BEAN—TOMATO SAUCE

1 (28-ounce) can crushed tomatoes with purée

1 cup chicken stock (see page 10)

$^1/_2$ cup dry sherry

3 tablespoons salted black beans, rinsed and
   coarsely chopped

1 tablespoon oyster sauce

1 tablespoon Asian sesame oil

1 tablespoon Vietnamese garlic-chile sauce

To prepare the lamb shanks, preheat the oven to 350°. Season the shanks with salt and pepper. Pour the peanut oil into a flameproof Dutch oven large enough to hold all 4 shanks, and heat over high heat until extremely hot. Spread the seasoned flour on a plate and dredge the shanks in it. Place in the hot pan and brown well on all sides. Remove the shanks. Decrease the heat to medium-high and add the garlic, celery, carrot, and onion and sauté for 3 minutes, until browned. Return the shanks to the pan, pour the stock over the shanks, and cover the dish. Place in the oven and cook for 1$^3/_4$ to 2 hours, until tender.

Meanwhile, prepare the sauce: Combine all the ingredients in a saucepan and place over medium-high heat. Bring to a boil, then decrease the heat to low and simmer, uncovered, for 20 minutes, until thickened. Keep warm.

Remove the shanks from the oven, transfer to a plate, and keep warm. Increase the oven temperature to 375°.

Add the sauce to the Dutch oven holding the vegetables and stock and cook for 5 minutes, until warmed. Add the shanks and cook for about 3 minutes, until heated through.

To assemble each serving, place a shank on a plate and ladle the sauce on top.

———————————————

SERVES 4

Dynamite Baked Opah

This is our version of what sushi bars call "dynamite." It's the dish by which many raw-fish novices are indoctrinated, because it is actually baked. The first-timers get hooked, and then move on to raw fish.

2 tablespoons unsalted butter

1/2 cup julienned yellow onion

3 cups stemmed and sliced shiitake mushrooms

1 cup good-quality mayonnaise

3/4 cup chopped green onion, white and green parts

2 tablespoons chopped fresh basil

1 1/2 teaspoons soy sauce

6 (6-ounce) thick opah or sea bass fillets

Salt

Freshly ground black pepper

1/2 cup dry white wine

1/4 cup tobiko (flying fish roe)

Preheat the oven to 400°.

In a sauté pan, melt the butter over medium heat. Add the yellow onion and mushrooms and sauté for 3 minutes, until softened. Remove from the heat and let cool.

In a bowl, combine the mushroom mixture, mayonnaise, green onion, basil, and soy sauce and mix well.

Season both sides of the fish with salt and pepper. Spray the bottom of baking dish with vegetable-oil cooking spray and place the fish fillets in the dish. Pour the wine over the fish, and then cover each fillet with an equal amount of the mayonnaise mixture.

Bake for 20 minutes, until the tops have browned and the fish is just cooked through. To serve, top each fillet with the tobiko and serve immediately.

SERVES 6

🗲 I don't believe the only mayonnaise is homemade mayonnaise. For my money, Best Foods—called Hellmann's east of the Rockies—is the best all-purpose mayonnaise you can buy.

Chinese Roast Duck with Mango-Apricot Sauce and Herbed Potato Lumpia

This presentation, which we put on the menu at Christmastime 1998, is the evolution of our duck dish over a dozen years. When we first started making it, we bought precooked duck from Maple Leaf Farms. It was good and it satisfied my requirement that the duck have crispy skin but not much fat. As I became more comfortable in the role of restaurant chef, I started cooking my own ducks. After much experimentation, I came up with a method of cooking the duck perfectly.

HERBED POTATO LUMPIA

6 cups peeled and cubed potatoes

2 tablespoons unsalted butter

2 tablespoons half-and-half

2 teaspoons salt

1/8 teaspoon pepper

1/4 cup chopped green onion, white part only

2 tablespoons chopped fresh cilantro

1 tablespoon chopped fresh chives

1 egg yolk

2 teaspoons water

6 (7-inch-square) lumpia wrappers

Peanut oil, for deep-frying

DUCK SPICE MIX

2 tablespoons Szechuan peppercorns

1 tablespoon coriander seeds

1 tablespoon black peppercorns

1 tablespoon star anise

1 tablespoon garlic powder

3 tablespoons kosher salt

1 tablespoon curry powder

3 (4- to 5-pound) ducks

MANGO-APRICOT SAUCE

2 cups cubed mango

3 cups chicken stock (see page 10)

1 lemongrass stalk, white part only, pounded

1 tablespoon peeled and minced fresh ginger

3 cloves garlic, minced

3 tablespoons apricot preserves

1 tablespoon freshly squeezed lime juice

To prepare the lumpia, in a large saucepan, combine the potatoes with salted water to cover and bring to a boil over medium-high heat. Cook for 15 minutes, until tender. Drain and place in a bowl. Add the butter and half-and-half and coarsely mash. Add the salt, pepper, green onion, cilantro, and chives and stir to mix.

To assemble the lumpia, in a small bowl, whisk together the egg yolk and water to form an egg wash. Lay out the lumpia wrappers, positioning each of them with a point facing you. Evenly divide the potato mixture and place it across the bottom of each wrapper, about 2 inches above the point. Fold the bottom up over the filling and fold in the sides toward the middle. Brush the unfolded edges with the egg wash. Starting at the bottom, roll up to form a tidy bundle. Repeat with the remaining filling and wrappers. Cover and chill for a few hours before frying.

Preheat the oven to 425°.

To prepare the spice mix, in a sauté pan, toast the Szechuan peppercorns, coriander seeds, black peppercorns, and star anise over medium-high heat for 3 to 4 minutes, until fragrant. Remove from the heat and let cool. Grind the toasted spices in a coffee grinder to the consistency of coarse salt and pour into a small bowl. Add the garlic powder, salt, and curry powder and mix well.

Prick the skin of each duck all over with a sharp knife. Rub generously with the spice mix. Place the ducks on a rack in a large roasting pan and roast for 15 minutes. Decrease the oven temperature to 350° and continue to roast for 1 hour and 15 minutes, until tender.

To make the sauce, in a saucepan, combine the mango, stock, lemongrass, ginger, garlic, and apricot preserves over medium-high heat. Cook for about 15 minutes, until reduced by half. Remove from the heat, discard the lemongrass, and purée the mixture in a food processor or blender. Stir in the lime juice. Keep warm.

To cook the lumpia, in a heavy saucepan, pour in the peanut oil to a depth of about 1 inch and heat to 375°. Add 2 lumpia and fry, turning with tongs to fry evenly, for $1^{1}/_{2}$ to 2 minutes, until crisp and browned. Using tongs or a wire skimmer, transfer to paper towels to drain. Repeat with the remaining lumpia.

To serve, cut each duck in half, removing the backbone and breastbone. Place each duck half along with 1 lumpia on each plate and spoon the mango-apricot sauce over the duck. Serve immediately.

SERVES 6

Paniolo Ribs with Hali‘imaile Barbecue Sauce and Coconut–Sweet Potato Cakes

HGS Classic

What can I say about the ribs? I'm from Texas! Anyone who grew up in Texas and cooks has his or her favorite rib recipe. And by the way, the flavor comes as much from the cooking of the ribs as it does from the sauce. These ribs have been on the menu since the day we opened. After twelve years of many creative items on our menu, these ribs still seem to be everyone's favorite.

Coconut–Sweet Potato Cakes

3 pounds Moloka‘i sweet potatoes (or other variety)

4 tablespoons unsalted butter, plus extra for sautéing

1 tablespoon sugar

1 teaspoon salt

1 teaspoon ground cinnamon

2 cups shredded dried coconut

Hali‘imaile Barbecue Sauce

2 tablespoons margarine

2 onions, chopped

3 cups ketchup

1 1/2 cups red chile sauce

1/2 cup cider vinegar

1/2 cup firmly packed brown sugar

1/3 cup prepared mustard

1/3 cup dark molasses

2 teaspoons cayenne pepper

1/3 cup Worcestershire sauce

2 teaspoons liquid smoke

Juice of 1/2 lemon

Juice of 1/2 lime

Juice of 1/2 orange

Salt

Freshly ground black pepper

6 racks baby back ribs (about 6 pounds total)

To prepare the sweet potato cakes, preheat the oven to 350°. Pierce the sweet potatoes with fork tines and place in the oven. Bake for about 45 minutes, until tender. When done, remove from the oven and, when cool enough to handle, cut the potatoes in half and scoop out the pulp. Pass the pulp through a food mill placed over a bowl. Add the butter, sugar, salt, and cinnamon and mix well. Cover and refrigerate for 2 hours, until firm.

To prepare the sauce, in a heavy saucepan, melt the margarine over medium heat. Add the onions and sauté for 5 to 6 minutes, until translucent. Add all the remaining ingredients and bring to a boil. Reduce the heat to low and simmer, uncovered, for 2 hours, until thick and reddish brown.

Increase the oven temperature to 400°. To prepare the ribs, place the rib racks in a roasting pan with the ribs in an upright position. Add water to cover, then cover the pan with aluminum foil. Bake for 1 hour. The ribs will be cooked through at this point.

Meanwhile, prepare a fire in a charcoal grill, or preheat a gas grill. When the ribs are ready, dip them in the barbecue sauce, and place on the prepared grill. Cook, turning once, for 3 minutes per side, until well marked.

Just before the ribs are ready, divide the sweet potato mixture into 12 equal portions. Form each portion into a patty about 1/2 inch thick and 2 1/2 inches in diameter. Coat the patties evenly with the coconut.

Decrease the oven temperature to 325°. In a large sauté pan, melt enough butter to coat the bottom of the pan. Add the patties, in batches if necessary, and sauté, turning once, for 4 minutes on each side, until golden brown. Transfer to a baking dish and place in the oven for 8 minutes, until heated through.

Cut each rib rack into thirds, and overlap the 3 portions on

individual plates. Spoon 2 tablespoons of the sauce over each serving and serve immediately. The remaining sauce can be stored for up to 3 weeks in an airtight container in the refrigerator.

Serves 6

❧ Everyone always asks us about the "secret" to our ribs. The secret is to bake and steam them rather than boil them.

GRILLED PORK TENDERLOIN
WITH GRILLED MUSHROOM POLENTA
AND FRESH PINEAPPLE CHUTNEY

When we first opened the "store," one of our takeout items was a marinated pork tenderloin. When we became a "restaurant" twenty-four hours later, it was a natural to have a pork dish on the menu. Over the years, we have rotated various pork items onto the menu. It's always a big seller, especially with our homemade pineapple chutney.

MARINADE

1 cup thawed, frozen orange juice concentrate

1/2 cup Dijon mustard

2 tablespoons dark rum

3 tablespoons dark molasses

6 tablespoons canola oil

2 teaspoons freshly ground black pepper

5 cloves garlic

1 teaspoon sambal (Indonesian garlic-chile paste)

1 teaspoon chopped fresh thyme

1 teaspoon chopped fresh rosemary

1 (2-pound) pork tenderloin

GRILLED MUSHROOM POLENTA

*1 tablespoon plus 1 1/2 teaspoons olive oil,
   plus extra for brushing*

2 cloves garlic, chopped

1/4 pound shiitake mushrooms, coarsely chopped

2 cups water

3 cups chicken stock (see page 10)

1 teaspoon salt

1 1/2 cups instant polenta

1 cup grated Parmesan cheese

FRESH PINEAPPLE CHUTNEY

2 tablespoons margarine

1 1/2 cups chopped onion

3 cups diced fresh pineapple

3/4 cup firmly packed dark brown sugar

1/2 cup rice vinegar

3 tablespoons chopped fresh basil

1 teaspoon sambal (Indonesian garlic-chile paste)

3/4 cup raisins

2 tablespoons peeled and grated fresh ginger

To prepare the marinade, in a bowl, combine all the ingredients and mix well. Place the tenderloin in a shallow dish and pour the marinade over the top. Cover and marinate for 2 to 4 hours in the refrigerator.

To prepare the polenta, in a skillet, heat the olive oil over medium-high heat. Add the garlic and mushrooms and sauté for 5 minutes, until tender.

Combine the water and stock in a large, heavy saucepan over medium-high heat and bring to a boil. Add the salt, then pour in the polenta in a stream, stirring constantly to prevent lumps. Continue to stir until smooth, then simmer for 5 to 8 minutes, until thick. Stir in the mushrooms and the Parmesan. Spray a 15 1/2 by 1/2-inch jelly-roll pan with vegetable-oil cooking spray. Spread the polenta evenly in the prepared pan and refrigerate for 2 hours, until set.

To prepare the chutney, in a skillet, melt the margarine over medium heat. Add the onion and sauté for 6 minutes, until translucent. Add all the remaining ingredients and cook for about 30 minutes, until thick and still chunky. Remove from the heat and allow to cool. (The chutney can be made up to 1 week in advance. Store in an airtight container in the refrigerator.)

Prepare a fire in a charcoal grill, or preheat a gas grill.

Cut the polenta into 3-inch squares, then cut the squares into triangles, and brush on both sides with olive oil. Remove the tenderloin from the marinade. Place the tenderloin on the grill rack and grill, turning as needed, for 7 to 8 minutes for medium rare. Transfer to a platter and let rest for 5 minutes, then slice on the diagonal into $1/4$-inch slices. Meanwhile, place the polenta triangles on the grill rack and grill, turning once, for 2 minutes on each side, until golden brown and heated through.

To serve, place 2 polenta triangles on each plate and fan 3 to 4 slices of tenderloin on top. Spoon the chutney over the pork and serve immediately.

SERVES 6

SEARED VENISON WITH DRIED CHERRY–PORT WINE SAUCE AND CRISPY ROQUEFORT POTATO CAKES

After many menu tastings, this dish won out as the main course for a client's millennial New Year's Eve party, the most extravagant party we've ever catered. It defied description, from sundial invitations to handmade black pottery plates rimmed in platinum. Everything about it was perfect down to the most minute detail. Definitely the party of a lifetime.

CRISPY ROQUEFORT POTATO CAKES

2^1/2 *cups peeled and cubed potatoes (*^{1}/2*-inch cubes)*

2 cloves garlic, smashed

2 tablespoons unsalted butter

2 tablespoons Roquefort cheese

^{1}/2 *teaspoon salt*

Pinch of freshly ground black pepper

1 tablespoon chopped fresh chives

1 tablespoon chopped green onion, green part only

^{1}/3 *cup fine dried bread crumbs*

1 tablespoon chopped fresh flat-leaf parsley

2 tablespoons unsalted butter, melted

1 (2-pound) rack of venison

^{1}/2 *cup port wine*

^{1}/2 *cup demi-glace (page 112)*

Salt

Freshly ground black pepper

1 tablespoon unsalted butter

1^1/2 *teaspoons chopped shallot*

^{1}/2 *cup dried cherries, coarsely chopped*

Thyme sprigs, for garnish

To prepare the potato cakes, in a saucepan combine the potatoes with water to cover. Add the garlic, bring to a boil, and boil for 10 to 12 minutes, until tender. Drain and discard the garlic. Place the hot potatoes in a bowl and toss with the butter, Roquefort cheese, salt, and pepper. Add the chives and green onion and mix well. Divide the mixture into 4 equal portions and press each portion into a 2^1/2-inch-round mold. Refrigerate for 1 hour, until set.

To prepare the venison, preheat the oven to 450°. Trim any excess fat or tendons from the loin. Remove the loin from the rack and set aside. Place the bones in a roasting pan and roast in the oven for 30 minutes, until very brown. Remove from the oven. Decrease the oven temperature to 350°.

Place the port in a saucepan over medium heat. Add the venison bones and simmer for 15 minutes, until reduced by one-half. Strain through a sieve into a clean saucepan and add the demi-glace. Place over low heat for about 15 minutes, until reduced by half.

Heat a nonstick sauté pan until very hot. Season both sides of the venison loin with salt and pepper. Add the loin to the pan and brown on all sides. Transfer the loin to a roasting pan and place in the oven. Roast for 25 minutes for medium rare, until the internal temperature reads 140 to 145° on a meat thermometer, or to desired doneness. Remove from the oven and increase the temperature to 425°.

In a sauté pan, melt the butter over medium heat. Add the shallot and sauté for 2 minutes, until translucent. Add the cherries and cook for 2 minutes. Decrease the heat to low, add 2 tablespoons of the reduced wine sauce, and cook for another 2 minutes. Add the cherry mixture to the rest of the wine sauce and

cook for 2 to 3 minutes, until the cherries are softened. If the sauce gets too thick, add another 1 tablespoon of the demi-glace.

To cook the potato cakes, remove from the refrigerator and gently release from the molds. In a small bowl, toss together the bread crumbs and parsley. Brush each cake with the melted butter. Press the bread crumb and parsley mixture on the top and sides of each cake. Spray a baking sheet with vegetable-oil cooking spray. Place the potato cakes on the prepared sheet and bake for 15 to 20 minutes, until golden brown and heated through.

To serve, place a potato cake on each plate. Slice the loin and lay 4 to 5 slices against each cake. Ladle 2 tablespoons of the port and cherry sauce over each serving.

SERVES 4

Tenderloin of Beef with
Lobster, Artichoke, and Mushroom Hash

This is a dish we make a lot for large group sit-down dinners. It's an easy entrée to "dish up" when you're in a tent in the middle of a field with no electricity or running water.

1 (2¹/2-pound) beef tenderloin

Extra virgin olive oil, for oiling meat

1 tablespoon chopped garlic

Salt

Freshly ground black pepper

Rosemary sprigs, for seasoning and garnish

Thyme sprigs, for seasoning and garnish

³/4 cup demi-glace (page 112)

LOBSTER, ARTICHOKE,
AND MUSHROOM HASH

3 tablespoons unsalted butter

3 tablespoons olive oil

1 pound lobster tail meat

2 cloves garlic, chopped

3 tablespoons chopped shallot

3 leeks, white part only, chopped

2 fennel bulbs, sliced lengthwise

¹/2 pound fresh shiitake mushrooms, sliced

¹/2 pound button mushrooms, sliced

3 large artichoke hearts, cooked and quartered (see note)

1 teaspoon chopped fresh chives

1 teaspoon chopped fresh rosemary

1 tablespoon fresh thyme leaves

12 cloves roasted garlic (page 9)

Salt

Freshly ground black pepper

Lightly rub the tenderloin with olive oil. Season with the garlic, salt, and pepper. Place some rosemary and thyme sprigs on the bottom of a roasting pan, place the tenderloin on top, and place a few sprigs of each herb on top of the tenderloin. Set aside for about 1 hour, until it reaches room temperature.

To prepare the hash, place 1¹/2 tablespoons each of the butter and oil in a large sauté pan over medium heat. Add the lobster meat and sauté for 3 to 5 minutes, until just cooked. Remove the lobster from the pan.

Add the remaining 1¹/2 tablespoons each butter and oil to the same pan. When melted, add the garlic, shallot, leeks, and fennel and sauté over medium-high heat for 6 to 8 minutes, until the fennel is barely fork tender. Add the mushrooms and artichokes and sauté over high heat for 5 to 6 minutes, until the liquid from the mushrooms evaporates. Add the lobster meat, sprinkle in the chives, rosemary, thyme, and roasted garlic, and toss. Season with salt and pepper. Keep warm until serving.

To cook the tenderloin, preheat the oven to 450°. Remove the tenderloin from the herbs and transfer to a roasting pan. Place in the oven and cook for 25 minutes for medium rare.

To assemble each serving, place a mound of the hash in the center of each plate. Slice the tenderloin and place slices on top of the hash. Heat the demi-glace and drizzle around the plate. Garnish with sprigs of rosemary and thyme. Serve immediately.

SERVES 6

To prepare your own fresh ARTICHOKE HEARTS, first wash the artichokes well. Remove the discolored outermost leaves, trim each leaf by about $^1/_4$ inch to remove any thorns, and cut the stem so that it is flush with the bottom leaves. In a large saucepan, combine the artichokes with water to cover, $^1/_4$ cup freshly squeezed lemon juice, and 2 teaspoons salt over high heat. Cover and bring to a boil. Decrease the heat to medium and boil for about 50 minutes, until tender. Drain the artichokes, and, when cool enough to handle, remove the tough outer leaves to expose the thin inner leaves that are green at the top but yellowish at the base. Trim off the top inch or so of the entire artichoke, then slice or quarter the remaining section, as the recipe calls for. Pull out the immature prickly, pinkish leaves in the center and use the tip of a spoon to scrape up the fuzz beneath, called the choke.

WHITE AND DARK CHOCOLATE MOUSSE CAKE

I brought this recipe home from La Gavroche in London, where I worked in 1985 and 1986. It's one of those standard, everyone-loves-chocolate-mousse kind of desserts. You'll need to make 1¹/₂ times the pastry cream recipe so you'll have an extra cup for the white chocolate mousse. — T.G.

PASTRY CREAM
MAKES 2 CUPS

2 cups milk
¹/₂ vanilla bean, split lengthwise
¹/₂ cup plus 1 teaspoon sugar
6 egg yolks, at room temperature
3 tablespoons cornstarch

CHOCOLATE FUDGE CAKE

¹/₄ cup cocoa powder
¹/₃ cup sour cream
1 egg
³/₄ teaspoon vanilla extract
³/₄ cup sifted cake flour
¹/₂ cup sugar
¹/₄ teaspoon baking soda
¹/₂ teaspoon baking powder
¹/₄ teaspoon salt
6 tablespoons unsalted butter, at room temperature

DARK CHOCOLATE MOUSSE
MAKES 3 CUPS

1¹/₂ cups heavy cream
8 ounces semisweet chocolate
6 tablespoons simple syrup (page 44)
4 egg yolks

RASPBERRY SAUCE
MAKES 1 CUP

¹/₂ pound frozen raspberries, thawed
¹/₂ cup simple syrup (page 44)
¹/₂ teaspoon freshly squeezed lemon juice

WHITE CHOCOLATE MOUSSE
MAKES 3 CUPS

1¹/₂ cups heavy cream
³/₄ pound white chocolate
1 cup pastry cream

¹/₄ cup simple syrup (page 44), for soaking

To prepare the pastry cream, pour the milk into a saucepan over medium heat. Scrape the seeds of the vanilla bean into the milk, then add the pods. Meanwhile, in a stainless-steel or other heatproof bowl, whisk together the sugar and egg yolks. Sift the cornstarch into the mixture.

When the milk comes to a boil, remove from the heat and remove the vanilla bean. Slowly ladle half of the milk into the yolks while whisking constantly. Return the mixture to the saucepan with the remaining milk and, whisking constantly, bring to a rolling boil. Pour into a bowl to cool. Cover with plastic wrap, pressing it directly onto the surface to prevent a skin from forming. Refrigerate for at least 3 hours or up to overnight.

To prepare the cake, preheat the oven to 350°. Mix together the cocoa, sour cream, egg, and vanilla. Set aside. In another bowl, sift together the flour, sugar, baking soda, baking powder, and salt. Add the butter and half of the cocoa mixture to the flour mixture and, using an electric mixer on medium speed, beat until blended. Scrape down the sides of the bowl. Slowly add the remaining cocoa mixture and beat for about 3 minutes, until completely incorporated.

Pour the batter into an ungreased 8 by 3-inch round cake pan and bake for 25 to 30 minutes, until a toothpick comes out clean. Remove from the oven and allow to cool for 30 minutes in the pan, then turn out of the pan and allow to cool completely on a rack. Using a serrated knife, cut in half horizontally to create 2 layers. Set aside 1 layer for this recipe. Reserve the other layer for another use (or eat it!).

To prepare the dark chocolate mousse, whip the cream to a ribbon stage. It should not be stiff, but should start to form a ribbon when dripped from a spatula. Cover and place in the refrigerator. Place the chocolate in the top pan of a double boiler over barely simmering water. When the chocolate is completely melted, remove from the heat.

In a saucepan, bring the simple syrup to a boil. Meanwhile, put the egg yolks in a stainless steel or other heatproof bowl. Pour the hot syrup into the yolks, whisking briskly. Place the bowl on top of a pan of boiling water and whip with a wire whisk until the mixture doubles in volume. Remove from the

(continued)

heat and beat with an electric mixer on medium speed for 5 minutes, until half cooled.

Pour the melted chocolate into the egg mixture, and, using an electric mixer on low speed, mix until the chocolate is incorporated. Scrape down the sides of the bowl. Fold in the whipped cream. Cover and refrigerate until needed.

To prepare the raspberry sauce, pour off half the liquid from the thawed berries and reserve. Purée the raspberries with the remaining liquid, the simple syrup, and the lemon juice. Strain through a fine-mesh sieve, cover, and refrigerate until serving.

To prepare the white chocolate mousse, whip the cream to the ribbon stage. Melt the chocolate in a double boiler as you did for the dark chocolate mouse. Pour the 1 cup pastry cream into a bowl. Using an electric mixer on medium speed, whip the pastry cream until it reaches room temperature. Slowly pour the melted white chocolate into the pastry cream, and mix until the chocolate is fully incorporated. Scrape down the sides of the bowl, then fold in the whipped cream. (Always prepare the white chocolate mousse last, because it will start to set.)

To assemble the cake, first select an 8 by 3-inch ring mold. Soak the chocolate cake in the reserved raspberry liquid and the 1/4 cup simple syrup, then place in the mold. Spoon in the dark chocolate mouse, half-filling the remaining space in the mold. Cover and place in the freezer for 1 hour. Remove from the freezer and top with the white chocolate mousse, filling the mold. Re-cover and freeze overnight.

To unmold, rinse a kitchen towel with hot water, wring it out well, and briefly hold it around the base of the mold. Alternatively, if you are more advanced, use a butane torch to warm the mold briefly. Invert a serving plate on top of the mold, and invert the plate and mold together. Lift off the mold and serve immediately with the raspberry sauce.

SERVES 8

🌿 The chocolate mousse has no egg whites, so it softens nicely and is very versatile. It can be kept in the refrigerator for up to 2 weeks. Be creative and use it for other recipes.

Warm Gingerbread with Mascarpone Filling and Sautéed Pears

I created this dessert expressly for a Turley Vineyards winemaker's dinner at the restaurant. The dinner was designed to showcase some of the best wines of this Napa Valley–based winery. We left the gingerbread on the menu for a month after the event, and often bring it back in the wintertime.—T.G.

Gingerbread

1¹/₂ cups hot water

1 cup light unsulphured molasses

1 teaspoon baking soda

¹/₂ cup unsalted butter, at room temperature

1 cup firmly packed brown sugar

1 egg

2¹/₄ cups flour

1 teaspoon baking powder

2 teaspoons ground ginger

1 teaspoon ground cinnamon

¹/₂ teaspoon ground cloves

¹/₂ teaspoon salt

Mascarpone Filling

2 cups mascarpone cheese

¹/₂ cup granulated sugar

2 tablespoons pear William or other pear liqueur

Sautéed Pears

2 tablespoons unsalted butter

3 large pears, peeled, halved, cored, and coarsely chopped

¹/₂ cup granulated sugar

2 tablespoons pear William or other pear liqueur

To prepare the gingerbread, preheat the oven to 350°. Butter and flour a 9 by 5¹/₂-inch loaf pan or 6 (4 by 2-inch) Bundt pans. In a bowl, combine the hot water, molasses, and baking soda and let stand for 10 minutes. In another bowl, using an electric mixer on low speed, cream together the butter and sugar. Add the egg and mix well. In a third bowl, sift together the flour, baking powder, ginger, cinnamon, cloves, and salt. Add the flour mixture to the butter mixture in 3 batches, alternating with the molasses mixture and beginning and ending with the flour mixture.

Pour the batter into the prepared pan(s). Bake for 45 to 50 minutes for a loaf pan or 20 to 25 minutes for Bundt pans, until a toothpick inserted into the center comes out clean. Remove from the oven (leaving the heat on) and turn the gingerbread(s) out of the pan(s). Allow to cool on a rack.

To prepare the filling, in a small bowl, mix together all the ingredients.

To prepare the pears, in a sauté pan, melt the butter over medium heat. Add the pears and sugar, increase the heat to medium-high, and sauté for 5 to 6 minutes, until light brown. Add the liqueur and remove from heat.

To assemble the dessert, if you have made 1 loaf, cut with a serrated knife into 6 equal pieces. Divide the slices or Bundt cakes among dessert plates. Spoon the mascarpone mixture evenly over each serving. Place the plates on a baking sheet, and heat in the oven for 7 to 10 minutes, until the mascarpone filling begins to melt.

Reheat the pears gently, if necessary, and spoon the pears and their liquid on top of the gingerbread. Serve immediately.

Serves 6

UNTITLED I

This is the dessert I created to replace the Chocolate Macadamia Nut Pie (page 190). I knew I had to come up with something stupendous, so I combined a whole bunch of rich ingredients: chocolate dough, macadamia nuts, caramel, bananas, more chocolate, chocolate mousse. It pacified our customers for a while, until they realized the pie was gone. We put the pie back on, but this tart had built up its own cadre of fans. So now we offer both. Several of us have tried to come up with a name for this one. The best we could do went something like Cheech's Chocolate Mac Nut, Caramel, Banana, Chocolate, Chocolate Mousse. So we settled on Untitled I for this artistic masterpiece.

Making your own caramel is a potentially dangerous situation. You can get burned, literally. But I say, "Oh, go ahead and try it!" Or, take the easy way out and buy a thick, good-quality caramel sauce. — *T.G.*

CARAMEL FILLING
MAKES 2 CUPS

2 cups sugar

1 cup water

1 cup heavy cream

3 tablespoons cold unsalted butter, cut into small pieces

1 recipe chocolate crust dough (page 190)

CRÈME ANGLAISE
MAKES 2¹/₂ CUPS

1 cup heavy cream

1 cup milk

¹/₂ vanilla bean, split lengthwise

¹/₂ cup sugar

6 egg yolks

1 cup chocolate ganache (page 192)

1 cup macadamia nuts, toasted (page 106)

2 large or 3 small bananas, peeled and sliced

2 cups dark chocolate mousse (page 184)

To prepare the caramel filling, in a saucepan, combine the sugar and water over medium heat. Bring to a boil and continue cooking for 10 to 15 minutes, until the mixture turns a light amber. Remove from the heat.

Add the cream very, very slowly to the caramelized sugar, mixing constantly with a long-handled whisk. Add the butter and mix until combined. Allow to cool completely, then cover and refrigerate for 2 to 3 hours.

Preheat the oven to 350°. Spray 8 (3-inch) tartlet pans with removable bottoms with vegetable-oil cooking spray. Divide the dough into 8 equal parts. Roll each one out to ¹/₄ inch thick and 4 inches in diameter. Carefully transfer each to a prepared pan and press firmly into the bottom and sides of the pan. Using a rolling pin, press down on the edges of the pans to trim off the excess dough. Refrigerate the lined pans for 20 minutes.

Line the pastry shells with aluminum foil. Bake for 15 minutes, until the pastry begins to pull away from the sides of the pan. Allow to cool, remove the foil, and bake for an additional 10 minutes, until light brown.

To prepare the crème anglaise, combine the cream and milk in a saucepan. Using the tip of a sharp knife, scrape the seeds of the vanilla bean into the milk, then add the pods. Add the sugar and place over medium heat. Bring just to a boil, stirring to dissolve the sugar. Meanwhile, place the egg yolks in a bowl. When the milk mixture comes to a boil, remove from the heat and ladle 2 spoonfuls into the yolks while whisking constantly. Return to the saucepan with the remaining milk mixture and continue cooking over medium heat, stirring constantly, for 3 to 5 minutes, until the mixture coats the back of a spoon. Pour through a fine-mesh sieve placed over a bowl. Then nest the bowl in a bowl of ice to cool.

To assemble the cake, heat the ganache until melted (a microwave is fine as long as you do it slowly to prevent it from breaking) and brush or spoon a small amount into the bottom of each tart shell. Put one-eighth of the macadamia nuts into each shell. Scoop $1/4$ cup of the caramel filling into each shell. Place 4 banana slices in each shell. Cover the bananas with 2 tablespoons of the ganache, or enough to cover the bananas. Spoon the mousse into a pastry bag fitted with a 2-inch star tip. Pipe rosettes on top of each tart (like this dessert really needs anything else!). But we're not through yet! Serve with a pool of crème anglaise under each tartlet.

SERVES 8

CHOCOLATE MACADAMIA NUT PIE
HGS CLASSIC

We've been serving this pie at the store since the day we opened. It has a life of its own. We once tried to take it off the menu and caused a mini revolt among our customers. We replaced it with something equally as good. It didn't matter! The pie started out with small pieces of macadamia nuts, but we now use either whole or half nuts. Beverly says it's much more flavorful this way.—T.G.

CHOCOLATE CRUST

3/4 cup unsalted butter, at room temperature

1/2 cup plus 1 teaspoon sugar

1 egg yolk

2 tablespoons plus 1 1/2 teaspoons heavy cream

1/2 teaspoon vanilla extract

2 cups cake flour

1/4 cup cocoa powder

1/4 teaspoon salt

FILLING

4 tablespoons unsalted butter

2 ounces semisweet chocolate

5 eggs

1 cup sugar

1 1/2 cups dark corn syrup

1 teaspoon vanilla extract

2 1/2 cups halved macadamia nuts

WHIPPED CREAM

1 cup heavy cream

2 tablespoons sugar

1 teaspoon vanilla extract

2 tablespoons chopped macadamia nuts, for garnish

🍃 I use Cocoa Barry and Callibaut chocolates in all my recipes, but you can substitute any high-quality semisweet chocolate.

To prepare the crust, in a bowl, using an electric mixer on low speed, cream the butter and sugar together. Add the egg yolk, cream, and vanilla and mix well. In another bowl, sift together the flour, cocoa, and salt. Mix the flour mixture with the wet ingredients until incorporated. Press into a square on a piece of plastic wrap, wrap in the plastic, and refrigerate for 1 to 2 hours.

Remove the dough from the refrigerator, unwrap, and knead on a floured work surface until the dough is pliable. If using a 10-inch fluted tart pan with a removable bottom, roll the dough out to 1/4 inch thick and 12 inches in diameter. Spray the tart pan with vegetable-oil cooking spray. Carefully transfer the dough to the prepared pan and press firmly into the bottom and sides of the pan. Using a rolling pin, press down on the pan edges to trim off the excess dough. If using individual 3-inch tartlet pans with removable bottoms, divide the dough into 8 equal parts. Roll each one out to 1/4 inch thick and 4 inches in diameter. Spray the tartlet pans with vegetable-oil cooking spray. Carefully transfer each dough round to a prepared tartlet pan and press firmly into the bottom and sides of the pans. Using a rolling pin, press down on the edges of the pans to trim off the excess dough. Refrigerate the lined tart or tartlet pans for 20 minutes.

Preheat the oven to 350°. Line the pastry shells with aluminum foil. Bake the 10-inch tart for 15 minutes, or the tartlets for 10 minutes, until the pastry begins to pull away from the sides of the pan. Remove the shells from the oven and allow to cool before removing the foil. Decrease the oven temperature to 300°.

To prepare the filling, in a small saucepan, melt the butter over low heat. Stir in the chocolate until completed melted. In a bowl, mix the eggs, sugar, and corn syrup together. Add the chocolate mixture to the egg mixture and mix well. Add the vanilla extract and mix well. Fold in the nuts.

Pour the filling into the prebaked shells. Bake the 10-inch

tart for about 1 hour and 20 minutes, or the tartlets for 35 to 40 minutes, until the filling puffs up in the center but is not cracked. Allow to cool on racks and then refrigerate for 2 hours to make unmolding easier.

To prepare the whipped cream, combine all the ingredients in a bowl, and whip with an electric mixer on high speed until stiff peaks form.

To unmold, remove the pan sides and slide the pie or tarts onto a serving plate. Serve the pie at room temperature with the whipped cream and chopped nuts.

MAKES 1 (10-INCH) PIE OR
8 INDIVIDUAL TARTS; SERVES 8

KONA COFFEE CHEESECAKE

I created this cake from the top down. I wanted a way to use Nicky Matichyn's big, fat chocolate-covered espresso beans. (Nicky owns and operates a very popular local coffeehouse called Maui Coffee Roasters.) I was practically addicted to them, and I also thought we needed a coffee dessert. So I made a combined chocolate and coffee cheesecake on an Oreo cookie crust. Those espresso beans? I'd found a place for them! I used them to decorate the top of the cake. — T.G.

CHOCOLATE GANACHE

MAKES 2 CUPS

1 cup heavy cream
8 ounces semisweet chocolate

OREO COOKIE CRUST

5 tablespoons unsalted melted butter
3 cups Oreo cookie crumbs

CHEESECAKE FILLING

1 pound cream cheese, at room temperature
1 cup sugar
1/3 cup sour cream
1 tablespoon coffee extract
2 eggs

CHOCOLATE FILLING

1/2 pound cream cheese, at room temperature
1/2 cup sugar
3 tablespoons sour cream
1 egg

Chocolate-covered espresso beans

To prepare the ganache, in a saucepan, heat the cream over medium heat until hot. Remove from the heat and stir in the chocolate until melted. Let cool, cover, and refrigerate overnight. When ready to use, heat the ganache until melted (a microwave is fine as long as you do it slowly to prevent it from breaking).

To prepare the crust, in a bowl, combine the butter and the cookie crumbs and mix to moisten. Spray a 9-inch fluted tart pan with a removable bottom with vegetable-oil cooking spray. Press the mixture into the bottom and sides of the prepared pan.

Preheat the oven to 300°. To prepare the cheesecake filling, in a bowl, using an electric mixer on low speed, cream together the cream cheese and sugar until fluffy. Mix in the sour cream, then the coffee extract. Scrape down the sides of the bowl and add the eggs, one at a time, beating well after each addition.

To prepare the chocolate filling, in a bowl, cream together the cream cheese and sugar. Mix in the sour cream. Add 4 tablespoons of the ganache and then the egg. Pour the cheesecake filling into the crust and spoon the chocolate mixture on top. Swirl the cheesecake and chocolate together with a knife to achieve a marble effect.

Bake for 1 hour. Turn off the oven and let the cheesecake sit in the oven for 1 1/2 hours longer. Remove from the oven, let cool completely, cover, and refrigerate for at least 4 to 5 hours, or up to overnight.

To unmold, remove the pan sides and slide the cake onto a serving plate. Spoon the remaining ganache into a pastry bag fitted with a 2-inch star tip and pipe rosettes decoratively on the top. Put a chocolate-covered espresso bean in the center of each rosette.

SERVES 6 TO 8

❧ The folks who make Oreos have finally gotten wise, and you can now buy boxes of Oreo cookie crumbs. But then there are no extra cookies to munch on while you're baking!

CHOCOLATE–BANANA CREAM PIE
WITH PEANUT BUTTER CRUST

This pie has become the signature dessert at my parents' second restaurant, Joe's Bar & Grill, which emphasizes hearty American food. Its creation was a collaborative effort between Beverly and me. She said, "What do you think about bananas with peanut butter?" I said, "What do you think about bananas and chocolate and peanut butter?" This is the delicious end result.—T.G.

PEANUT BUTTER CRUST

4 tablespoons unsalted butter, at room temperature

1/4 cup granulated sugar

1/4 cup firmly packed dark brown sugar

1/4 cup crunchy peanut butter

1 egg

1 teaspoon vanilla extract

1/4 cup dry-roasted peanuts, coarsely chopped

3/4 cup flour

1/2 teaspoon baking powder

1/2 teaspoon baking soda

1/2 teaspoon salt

2 large bananas, peeled and sliced

1 cup chocolate ganache (page 192)

1 1/2 cups pastry cream (page 184)

2 cups dark chocolate mousse (page 184)

To prepare the dough, in a bowl, using an electric mixer on medium speed, cream together the butter and sugars. Add the peanut butter, egg, vanilla, and peanuts and mix well. In another bowl, sift together the flour, baking powder, baking soda, and salt. Add the flour mixture to the butter mixture and mix just until incorporated. Do not overmix. Cover and refrigerate for 1 hour.

Preheat the oven to 325°. Spray an 8-inch fluted tart pan with a removable bottom with vegetable-oil cooking spray. Roll the dough out to 1/4 inch thick and 10 inches in diameter; this may be difficult due to the peanuts. Carefully transfer the dough to the prepared pan and press firmly into the bottom and sides of the pan. Don't be alarmed if the dough cracks, simply press it back into shape. Using a rolling pin, press down on the pan edges to trim off the excess dough. Cover and refrigerate for 20 minutes. Bake for 20 to 25 minutes, until golden brown. Let cool on a rack and remove from the pan by removing the pan sides and sliding the crust onto a plate.

Line the pastry shell with the banana slices. Heat the ganache until melted (a microwave is fine as long as you do it slowly to prevent it from breaking). Reserve 2 tablespoons of the ganache for garnish, then pour the remainder over the top of the bananas, making sure you cover all the bananas. Cover and refrigerate for 30 minutes, until the ganache is set. Spoon the pastry cream into a pastry bag fitted with a plain 1/2-inch pastry tip. Pipe the pastry cream on top of the ganache. Remove the mousse from the refrigerator and soften with a spatula. Rinse out the pastry bag and spoon the mousse into the bag fitted with a 2-inch star tip. Pipe 5 large rosettes on top of the pastry cream. Drizzle the reserved ganache on top of the mousse. Without covering, refrigerate for 30 minutes before serving.

SERVES 6 TO 8

CHOCOLATE BREAD PUDDING

*I really wanted to do a bread pudding. I thought chocolate bread pudding would be a great varia-
tion, and that Hawaiian sweet bread would be the perfect base. I decided to make my own sweet
bread, which is similar to brioche. If you don't want to make your own bread, you can use any sturdy
sweet egg bread. You'll notice that this recipe uses a lot of cream. There's nothing "lo-cal" about it,
but it's sinfully yummy. It has become another dessert we can't take off the menu.—T.G.*

SWEET BREAD

2 tablespoons active dry yeast

3 cups flour

1/4 cup sugar

1 tablespoon salt

4 eggs

3 tablespoons milk

1 cup plus 2 tablespoons unsalted butter,
   at room temperature

1 egg yolk

CHOCOLATE FILLING

6 cups heavy cream

1 cup sugar

1 teaspoon vanilla extract

10 ounces semisweet chocolate, chopped

6 whole eggs plus 6 egg yolks

2 ounces semisweet chocolate, chopped

1 cup caramel filling (page 188), heated and melted

To prepare the sweet bread, in the following order, combine the yeast, flour, sugar, and salt in the bowl of a stand mixer.
Add the eggs and 1 tablespoon of the milk. Using the dough
hook, mix on low speed until a dough forms, then knead the
dough in the mixer for 15 minutes. Slowly add the butter and
continue to mix for an additional 15 to 20 minutes, until the
dough starts to snap against the side of the bowl. Remove from
the bowl, lightly wrap with plastic wrap, and place in the
refrigerator for at least 6 hours or up to overnight.

Spray a loaf pan with vegetable-oil cooking spray. Remove
the dough from the refrigerator, form it into a loaf, and place in
the prepared pan. Let rise at room temperature or hotter for 2 to
3 hours, until the dough rises to about 1 inch above the pan sides.

Preheat the oven to 350°. In a small bowl, whisk together
the remaining 2 tablespoons milk and the egg yolk to form a
wash. Brush the loaf with the egg wash and bake for 40 minutes,
until golden brown. Remove from the oven and immediately
invert out of the pan onto a rack. Allow to cool completely.

To prepare the filling, in a saucepan, combine the cream,
sugar, and vanilla and bring just to a boil over medium heat.
Remove from the heat and stir in the chocolate until melted.

Place the whole eggs and yolks in a bowl. Slowly ladle the
chocolate mixture into the eggs, while whisking constantly.

Preheat the oven to 300°. Cut the bread into 2-inch cubes
and place in a large bowl. Pour the chocolate mixture through a
sieve held over the bread, then mix carefully. Let the mixture sit
for 10 minutes, so the bread soaks up the filling.

Butter a 9 by 13-inch baking dish, then line the bottom with
parchment paper. Pour the bread mixture into the dish.
Sprinkle the chopped chocolate on top. Bake for 30 to 40 minutes, until the pudding is set. Remove from the oven, let cool,
and serve with the warm caramel filling.

SERVES 8

Well, well, well.
We've gone through a whole year of recipes
and no crab dip. Keep reading.

My Final Word

🌷

When I die, I'm going to have the crab dip recipe
chiseled on my tombstone. It's my way of ensuring
I'll have lots and lots of visitors. Until then . . .

Index